TEXAS BOUND

19 TEXAS STORIES

EDITED BY *Kay Cattarulla*

Southern Methodist University Press
Dallas

Requests for permission to reproduce material from this work should be
sent to:
    Permissions
    Southern Methodist University Press
    SMU Box 415
    Dallas, Texas 75275

Library of Congress Cataloging-in-Publication Data

Texas bound : 19 Texas stories / edited by Kay Cattarulla. — 1st ed.
        p.   cm. — (Southwest life and letters)
    ISBN 0–87074–367–8 (cloth) — ISBN 0–87074–368–6 (pbk.)
    1. American fiction—Texas.   2. American fiction—20th century.
I. Cattarulla, Kay.   II. Series.
PS659.T4   1994
813'.01089764—dc20   93–45385

Cover photograph *Texas* 1965 by Lee Friedlander,
courtesy of Fraenkel Gallery, San Francisco.

10 9 8 7 6 5 4 3

Copyright acknowledgments for reprinted stories appear on pages 243
and 244.

Texas Bound

SOUTHWEST LIFE AND LETTERS

A series designed to publish outstand-
ing new fiction and nonfiction about
Texas and the American Southwest and
to present classic works of the region in
handsome new editions.

General Editors: Kathryn Lang, Southern Methodist University Press; Tom
Pilkington, Tarleton State University

★

CONTENTS

Preface

S ince 1992, Texas actors have been reading Texas stories to a theater audience as part of the literary series "Arts and Letters Live" at the Dallas Museum of Art. Out of the great success of these readings has come the impulse to publish this book, which collects nearly all the short fiction featured to date in the project, "Texas Bound."

The stories were chosen by me, as producer, in collaboration with Randy Moore, who directs the "Texas Bound" readings. We tried to include as many important writers as possible and to provide a range of mood, voice, subject matter, and setting among the selections. We regretfully excluded many good pieces that we felt couldn't be read aloud successfully because of length or other reasons. In three instances—"Escape," "Good Rockin' Tonight," and "Major Six Pockets"—we went ahead with longer work which was cut for reading purposes.

The author's permission was obtained in each case and the uncut versions are restored for this book. It should be noted that two pieces, "Escape" and "Burgers, Beer, and Patsy Cline," are actually nonfiction.

The hours spent searching out these stories made me appreciate other anthologists of Texas short fiction, especially Don Graham and Suzanne Comer, some of whose choices—in *South by Southwest* and *Common Bonds* respectively—show up here. Material has also come from periodicals and short fiction collections that don't dwell exclusively on Texas and from authors not ordinarily thought of as "Texas writers." Every piece, however, has its origin in the state in one way or another. It's been a pleasure to bring them together.

SMU Press is also issuing eight of the "Texas Bound" readings on audiocassette.* The book and tape combination may be useful to those who work or teach in the small but lively field of literary performance. Anyone who does this, and anyone who loves short stories, should also become familiar with "Selected Shorts," produced in its live, public radio, and audiocassette versions by Symphony Space in New York City. "Selected Shorts"—which I initiated in 1985, in collaboration with Isaiah Sheffer, artistic director of Symphony Space—began the practice of inviting actors to read short fiction on stage, and has brought it to a national audience.

This "Texas Bound" offshoot and "Arts and Letters Live" as a whole have benefitted from the skill and encouragement of

---

*These are Larry McMurtry's "There Will Be Peace in Korea," read by Tommy Lee Jones; William Goyen's "The Texas Principessa," read by Doris Roberts; Robert Flynn's "The Midnight Clear," read by Tess Harper; Reginald McKnight's "The Kind of Light That Shines on Texas," read by Tyress Allen; Lynna Williams's "Personal Testimony," read by Judith Ivey; Tomás Rivera's "Picture of His Father's Face," read by Roger Alvarez; Annette Sanford's "Trip in a Summer Dress," read by Norma Moore; and Lawrence Wright's "Escape," read by Randy Moore. Published as *Texas Bound, 8 by 8: Stories by Texas Writers, Read by Texas Actors* (two 90-minute audiocassettes) by Southern Methodist University Press.

many people, particularly Melissa Berry, Director of Special Programs at the Dallas Museum of Art, and Lisa Taylor, expert publicist and associate producer. The Friends of the Dallas Public Library co-presented the series under two presidents, Sandra Melton and Susan Stahl.

Other notable help came from Kay Johnson, Stone Savage, and George Danielson of the Museum staff, and Frances Bell of the Dallas Public Library. Freda Gail Stern and Susan Teegardin provided key assists in the first season. Katherine Minton, Symphony Space's producer of literary programs, supplied endless advice and information, and the professional services of Russell Coleman, Sara Albert, Keith Gregory, Kathryn Lang, Freddie Goff, Bradley Hundley, and Nancy Lamb are gratefully acknowledged.

The actors who made it work (and made it fun) are Tyress Allen, Roger Alvarez, G. W. Bailey, Esther Benson, Alex Burton, Cora Cardona, Linda Gehringer, Tess Harper, Sean Hennigan, Judith Ivey, Tommy Lee Jones, Norma Moore, Doris Roberts, Nance Williamson, and especially the series host and director, Randy Moore.

"Arts and Letters Live" was made possible by a major grant from the Lila Wallace–Reader's Digest Fund. Additional support was provided by *The Dallas Morning News* as media sponsor and by the Texas Commission on the Arts.

Thanks to all, and above all to the writers who contributed their work.

Kay Cattarulla

Foreword

In 1938, Helena Huntington Smith was wandering around Montana and Wyoming, researching a novel about the Old West, when she came upon an elderly, weatherbeaten, but still clear-eyed and loquacious ex–Texas cowhand named E. C. Abbott, better known from Texas to Alberta as Teddy Blue. Over a period of days he related his stories about the great cattle drives from Texas to Montana and Nebraska in the latter part of the nineteenth century. Ms. Smith had the good sense not only to listen to these stories but also to *hear* them and to recognize them as literature. Thanks to the notes she made in the last months of Abbott's life, we have *We Pointed Them North: Recollections of a Cowpuncher,* which is a classic in the literature of Texas and the West.

You may ask: What kind of literature is it? After all, it is only a colorful cowboy's oral history, decorated by his imagination and the sympathetic narrative of memory. Certainly it doesn't compare in sophistication and technique with the work collected in this volume. The quality of writing available here is a testament to the maturing of Texas letters in the half-century since Teddy Blue spun out his tales. His stories, however, are the bedrock of the Texas cultural experience. They are primitive but intensely alive and bear the distinguishing marks of a culture that has a sense of its own apartness. It's exactly these qualities that make them literature.

In an essay in *Texas Monthly,* I argued that there are three levels of culture. We can recognize Level One in the Texas stereotype: the boasting, swaggering, rough-hewn, macho, materialistic, crass, and grasping qualities that the entire world associates with Texas. The virtues that attend these vices are self-assurance, courage, optimism, innovation, pragmatism, and a furious need for progress.

Level Two is the stage of sophistication, education, and neurosis. Embarrassed and secretly frightened by the energy of Level One, Level Two seeks asylum in the more civilized world. This is the period Texas letters has been in since the sixties, when the gates of culture opened and nearly every writer in the state fled to New York, Washington, or some European haunt, following a trend set by O. Henry and Katherine Anne Porter. Level Two is a necessary stage every great culture must pass through.

Every great writer must pass through it himself. Larry L. King, who dropped out of Texas Tech, made a classic excursion into Level Two when he wrote a novel set in Paris (France, not Texas)—a city he has never visited, to this very day. Larry McMurtry began his career by writing about exactly these powerful themes of cultural transition. His early work is represented here in his resonant 1964 story "There Will Be Peace in Korea," which is the basis for his novel *The Last Picture Show.* One can trace McMurtry's own journey through Level Two by his move to Georgetown and through the characters in his novels, who became increasingly cosmopolitan and less and less recognizably Texan. McMurtry painted a portrait of himself in this stage as he undertook a trip through Texas for *The Atlantic* in 1975, eating chicken-fried steak in Panhandle roadhouses as he read Euclides da Cunha's *Os Sertões*. Level Two writing is aimed at the condescending Eastern gentility, and here McMurtry holds Texas up for their examination and amusement. "Someday, I hope, teams of scholars will bestow upon the bardic tales and local myths of Texas the same quality of critical finesse that they are even now devoting to the Yugoslav epics," McMurtry wrote. "When they do, the first thing I expect them to note is that the state has had no Homer. Many bards, yes; innumerable village raconteurs, yes; and even, arguably, a few decent writers; but no Homer, and no Faulkner, either. Thus it has no single, greatly told tragic story, no central myth; and, lacking the historical identity that such a story provides, Texas in effect has no vital past." It is a testament both to McMurtry's skill and to his disguised ambition that he was able to recognize the great role that was waiting for him, once he made his peace with the culture that made McMurtry.

That is the business of Level Three: reconciliation. This is the stage where the artist, now educated to his craft and the sensibilities of the wider world, returns to the juicy roots of his own culture. The raw material of the tales of Teddy Blue is rediscovered and refined into the high art of McMurtry's epic, *Lonesome Dove*. In the process, an authentic literature is created. The great period of Texas literature announced itself with *Lonesome Dove* and Cormac McCarthy's *All the Pretty Horses*. Our Homer and Faulkner are writing today. These writers, as well as many others, are raising Texas letters to a higher point than even Texans ever imagined.

Perhaps that's why it required a New Yorker to recognize the present quality of Texas literature—and Kay Cattarulla certainly knows quality. As originator of National Public Radio's "Selected Shorts," Kay has a true ear for art and a devotion to excellence. Since 1992, she has put a spotlight on Texas writers through the "Texas Bound" readings at the Dallas Museum of Art, and in the process she has cultivated the vital audience that makes great writing prosper. This book belongs to Kay as much as it does to any writer in it. We all say thanks.

Lawrence Wright

Texas Bound

★

RICK BASS

Antlers

Halloween brings us all closer, in the valley. The Halloween party at the saloon is when we all, for the first time since last winter, realize why we are all up here—all three dozen of us— living in this cold, blue valley. Sometimes there are a few tourists through the valley in the high green grasses of summer, and the valley is opened up a little. People slip in and out of it; it's almost a regular place. But in October the snows come, and it closes down. It becomes our valley again, and the tourists and less hardy-of-heart people leave.

Everyone who's up here is here because of the silence. It is eternity up here. Some are on the run, and others are looking for something; some are incapable of living in a city, among people, while others simply love the wildness of new un- touched country. But our lives are all close enough, our feel- ings, that when winter comes in October there's a feeling like a sigh, a sigh after the great full meal of summer, and at the Halloween party everyone shows up, and we don't bother with costumes because we all know one another so well, if not through direct contact then through word of mouth—what Dick said Becky said about Don, and so forth—knowing more in this manner, sometimes. And instead of costumes, all we do is strap horns on our heads—moose antlers, or deer antlers, or even the high throwback of elk antlers—and we have a big potluck supper and get drunk as hell, even those of us who do not drink, that one night a year, and we dance all night long, putting nickels in the jukebox (Elvis, the Doors, Marty Robbins) and clomping around in the bar as if it were a dance floor, tables and stools set outside in the falling snow to make room, and the men and women bang their antlers against each other in mock battle. Then around two or three in the morning we all drive home, or ski home, or snowshoe home, or ride back on horses—however we got to the party is how we'll return.

It usually snows big on Halloween—a foot, a foot and a half. Sometimes whoever drove down to the saloon will give the skiers a ride home by fastening a long rope to the back bumper, and we skiers will hold on to that rope, still wearing our antlers, too drunk or tired to take them off, and we'll ride home that way, being pulled up the hill by the truck, gliding silently over the road's hard ice across the new snow, our heads tucked against the wind, against the falling snow . . .

Like children being let off at a bus stop, we'll let go of the rope when the truck passes our dark cabins. It would be nice to leave a lantern burning in the window, for coming home, but you don't ever go to sleep or leave with a lantern lit like that—it can burn your cabin down in the night and leave you in the middle of winter with nothing. We come home to dark houses, all of us. The antlers feel natural after having been up there for so long. Sometimes we bump them against the door going in and knock them off. We wear them only once a year: only once a year do we become the hunted.

We believe in this small place, this valley. Many of us have come here from other places and have been running all our lives from other things, and I think that everyone who is up here has decided not to run anymore.

There is a woman up here, Suzie, who has moved through the valley with a regularity, a rhythm, that is all her own and has nothing to do with our—the men's—pleadings or desires. Over the years, Suzie has been with all the men in this valley. All, that is, except Randy. She won't have anything to do with Randy. He still wishes very much for his chance, but because he is a bowhunter—he uses a strong compound bow and wicked, heart-gleaming aluminum arrows with a whole spindle of razor blades at one end for the killing point—she will have nothing to do with him.

Sometimes I wanted to defend Randy, even though I strongly disagreed with bowhunting. Bowhunting, it seemed to me, was wrong—but Randy was just Randy, no better or worse than any of the rest of us who had dated Suzie. Bowhunting was just something he did, something he couldn't help; I didn't see why she had to take it so personally.

Wolves eviscerate their prey; it's a hard life. Dead's dead, isn't it? And isn't pain the same everywhere?

I would say that Suzie's boyfriends lasted, on the average, three months. Nobody ever left her. Even the most sworn bachelors among us enjoyed her company—she worked at the bar every evening—and it was always Suzie who left the men, who left us, though I thought it was odd and wonderful that she never left the valley.

Suzie has sandy-red hair, high cold cheeks, and fury-blue eyes; she is short, no taller than anyone's shoulders. But be-cause most of us had known her for so long—and this is what the other men had told me after she'd left them—it was fun, and even stirring, but it wasn't really that *great*. There wasn't a lot of heat in it for most of them—not the dizzying, lost feeling kind you get sometimes when you meet someone for the first time, or even glimpse them in passing, never to meet. . . . That kind of heat was missing, said most of the men, and it was just comfortable, they said—*comfortable*.

When it was my turn to date Suzie, I'm proud to say that we stayed together for five months—longer than she's ever stayed with anyone—long enough for people to talk, and to kid her about it.

Our dates were simple enough; we'd go for long drives to the tops of snowy mountains and watch the valley. We'd drive into town, too, seventy miles away down a one-lane, rutted, cliff-hanging road, just for dinner and a movie. I could see how there was not heat and wild romance in it for some of the other men, but for me it was warm, and *right*, while it lasted.

When she left, I did not think I would ever eat again, drink again. It felt like my heart had been torn from my chest, like my lungs were on fire; every breath burned. I couldn't understand why she had to leave; I didn't know why she had to do that to me. I'd known it was coming, someday, but still it hurt. But I got over it; I lived. She's lovely. She's a nice girl. For a long time, I wished she would date Randy.

Besides being a bowhunter, Randy was a carpenter. He did odd jobs for people in the valley, usually fixing up old cabins rather than ever building any new ones. He kept his own schedule, and stopped working entirely in the fall so that he could hunt to his heart's content. He would roam the valley for days, exploring all of the wildest places, going all over the valley. He had hunted everywhere, had seen everything in the valley. We all hunted in the fall—grouse, deer, elk, though we left the moose and bear alone because they were rarer and we liked seeing them—but none of us were clever or stealthy enough to bowhunt. You had to get so close to the animal, with a bow.

Suzie didn't like any form of hunting. "That's what cattle are for," she'd say. "Cattle are like city people. Cattle expect, even deserve, what they've got coming. But wild animals are different. Wild animals enjoy life. They live in the woods on purpose. It's cruel to go in after them and kill them. It's cruel."

We'd all hoo-rah her and order more beers, and she wouldn't get angry, then—she'd understand that it was just what everyone did up here, the men and the women alike, that we loved the animals, loved seeing them, but that for one or two months out of the year we loved to hunt them. She couldn't understand it, but she knew that was how it was.

Randy was so good at what he did that we were jealous, and we admired him for it, tipped our hats to his talent. He could crawl right up to within thirty yards of wild animals when they were feeding, or he could sit so still that they would walk right past him. And he was good with his bow—he was deadly. The animal he shot would run a short way with the arrow stuck through it. An arrow wouldn't kill the way a bullet did, and the animal always ran at least a little way before dying—bleeding to death, or dying from trauma—and no one liked for that to happen, but the blood trail was easy to follow, especially in the snow. There was nothing that could be done about it; that was just the way bowhunting was. The men looked at it as being much fairer than hunting with a rifle, because you had to get so close to the animal to get a good shot—thirty-five, forty yards was the farthest away you could be—but Suzie didn't see it that way.

She would serve Randy his drinks and would chat with him, would be polite, but her face was a mask, her smiles were stiff.

What Randy did to try to gain Suzie's favor was to build her things. Davey, the bartender—the man she was dating that summer—didn't really mind. It wasn't as if there were any threat of Randy stealing her away, and besides, he liked the objects Randy built her; and, too, I think it might have seemed to add just the smallest bit of that white heat to Davey and Suzie's relationship—though I can't say that for sure.

Randy built her a porch swing out of bright larch wood and stained it with tung oil. It was as pretty as a new truck; he brought it up to her at the bar one night, having spent a week sanding it and getting it just right. We all gathered around, admiring it, running our hands over its smoothness. Suzie smiled a little—a polite smile, which was, in a way, worse than if she had looked angry—and said nothing, not even "thank you," and she and Davey took it home in the back of Davey's truck. This was in June.

Randy built her other things, too—small things, things she could fit on her dresser: a little mahogany box for her earrings, of which she had several pairs, and a walking stick with a deer's antler for the grip. She said she did not want the walking stick, but would take the earring box.

Some nights I would lie awake in my cabin and think about how Suzie was with Davey, and then I would feel sorry for Davey, because she would be leaving him eventually. I'd lie there on my side and look out my bedroom window at the northern lights flashing above the snowy mountains, and their strange light would be reflected on the river that ran past my cabin, so that the light seemed to be coming from beneath the water as well. On nights like those I'd feel like my heart was never going to heal—in fact, I was certain that it never would. I didn't love Suzie anymore—didn't think I did, anyway—but I wanted to love someone, and to be loved. Life, on those nights, seemed shorter than anything in the world, and so important, so precious, that it terrified me.

Perhaps Suzie was right about the bowhunting, and about all hunters.

In the evenings, back when we'd been together, Suzie and I would sit out on the back porch after she got in from work—still plenty of daylight left, the sun not setting until very late—and we'd watch large herds of deer, their antlers covered with summer velvet, wade out into the cool shadows of the river to bathe, like ladies. The sun would finally set, and those deer bodies would take on the dark shapes of the shadows, still out in the shallows of the rapids, splashing and bathing. Later, well into the night, Suzie and I would sit in the same chair, wrapped up in a single blanket, and nap. Shooting stars would shriek and howl over the mountains as if taunting us.

This past July, Randy, who lives along a field up on the side of the mountains at the north end of the valley up against the brief foothills, began practicing: standing out in the field at various marked distances—ten, twenty, thirty, forty yards—and shooting arrow after arrow into the bull's-eye target that was stapled to bales of hay. It was unusual to drive past in July and not see him out there in the field, practicing—even in the middle of the day, shirtless, perspiring, his cheeks flushed. He lived by himself, and there was probably nothing else to do. The bowhunting season began in late August, months before the regular gun season.

Too many people up here, I think, just get comfortable and lazy and lose their real passions—for whatever it is they used to get excited about. I've been up here only a few years, so maybe I have no right to say that, but it's what I feel.

It made Suzie furious to see Randy out practicing like that. She circulated a petition in the valley, requesting that bowhunting be banned.

But we—the other men, the other hunters—would have been doing the same thing, hunting the giant elk with bows for the thrill of it, luring them in with calls and rattles, right in to us, hidden in the bushes, the bulls wanting to fight, squealing madly and rushing in, tearing at trees and brush with their great dark antlers. If we could have gotten them in that close before killing them, we would have, and it would be a thing we would remember longer than any other thing. . . .

We just weren't good enough. We couldn't sign Suzie's petition. Not even Davey could sign it.

"It's wrong," she'd say.

"It's personal choice," Davey would say. "If you use the

7

meat, and apologize to the spirit right before you do it and right after—if you give thanks—it's okay. It's a man's choice, honey," he'd say—and if there was one thing Suzie hated, it was that man-woman stuff.

"He's trying to prove something," she said.

"He's just doing something he cares about, dear," Davey said.

"He's trying to prove his manhood—to me, to all of us," she said. "He's dangerous."

"No," said Davey, "that's not it. He likes it and hates it both. It fascinates him is all."

"It's sick," Suzie said. "He's dangerous."

I could see that Suzie would not be with Davey much longer. She moved from man to man almost with the seasons. There was a wildness, a flightiness, about her—some sort of combination of strength and terror—that made her desirable. To me, anyway, though I can only guess for the others.

I'd been out bowhunting with Randy once to see how it was done. I saw him shoot an elk, a huge bull, and I saw the arrow go in behind the bull's shoulder where the heart and lungs were hidden—and I saw, too, the way the bull looked around in wild-eyed surprise, and then went galloping off through the timber, seemingly uninjured, running hard. For a long time Randy and I sat there, listening to the clack-clack of the aluminum arrow banging against trees as the elk ran away with it.

"We sit and wait," Randy said. "We just wait." He was confident and did not seem at all shaky, though I was. It was a record bull, a beautiful bull. We sat there and waited. I did not believe we would ever see that bull again. I studied Randy's cool face, tiger-striped and frightening with the camouflage painted on it, and he seemed so cold, so icy.

After a couple of hours we got up and began to follow the blood trail. There wasn't much of it at all, at first—just a drop or two, drops in the dry leaves, already turning brown and cracking, drops that I would never have seen—but after about a quarter of a mile, farther down the hill, we began to see more of it, until it looked as if entire buckets of blood had been lost. We found two places where the bull had lain down beneath a tree to die, but had then gotten up and moved on again. We found him by the creek, a half mile away, down in the shadows, but with his huge antlers rising into a patch of sun and gleaming. He looked like a monster from another world; even after his death, he looked noble. The creek made a beautiful trickling sound. It was very quiet. But as we got closer, as large as he was, the bull looked like someone's pet. He looked friendly. The green-and-black arrow sticking out of him looked as if it had hurt his feelings more than anything; it did not look as if such a small arrow could kill such a large and strong animal.

We sat down beside the elk and admired him, studied him. Randy, who because of the scent did not smoke during the hunting season—not until he had his elk—pulled out a pack of cigarettes, shook one out, and lit it.

"I'm not sure why I do it," he admitted, reading my mind. "I feel kind of bad about it each time I see one like this, but I keep doing it." He shrugged. I listened to the sound of the creek. "I know it's cruel, but I can't help it. I have to do it," he said.

"What do you think it must feel like?" Suzie had asked me at the bar. "What do you think it must feel like to run around with an arrow in your heart, knowing you're going to die for it?" She was furious and righteous, red-faced, and I told her I didn't know. I paid for my drink and left, confused because she was right. The animal had to be feeling pain—serious, continuous pain. It was just the way it was.

In July, Suzie left Davey, as I'd predicted. It was gentle and kind—amicable—and we all had a party down at the saloon to celebrate. We roasted a whole deer that Holger Jennings had hit with his truck the night before while coming back from town with supplies, and we stayed out in front of the saloon and ate steaming fresh meat on paper plates with barbecue sauce and crisp apples from Idaho, and watched the lazy little river that followed the road that ran through town. We didn't dance or play loud music or anything—it was too mellow. There were children and dogs. This was back when Don Ter-linde was still alive, and he played his accordion: a sad, sweet sound. We drank beer and told stories.

All this time, I'd been uncertain about whether it was right or wrong to hunt if you used the meat and said those prayers. And I'm still not entirely convinced, one way or the other. But I do have a better picture of what it's like now to be the elk or deer. And I understand Suzie a little better, too: I no longer think of her as cruel for hurting Randy's proud heart, for sin-gling out, among all the other men in the valley, only Randy to shun, to avoid.

She wasn't cruel. She was just frightened. Fright—some-times plain fright, even more than terror—is every bit as bad as pain, and maybe worse.

What I am getting at is that Suzie went home with me that night after the party; she had made her rounds through the men of the valley, had sampled them all (except for Randy and a few of the more ancient ones), and now she was choosing to come back to me.

"I've got to go somewhere," she said. "I hate being alone. I can't stand to be alone." She slipped her hand in mine as we were walking home. Randy was still sitting on the picnic table with Davey when we left, eating slices of venison. The sun still hadn't quite set. Ducks flew down the river.

"I guess that's as close to 'I love you' as I'll get," I said.

"I'm serious," she said, twisting my hand. "You don't un-derstand. It's *horrible*. I can't *stand* it. It's not like other peo-ple's loneliness. It's worse."

"Why?" I asked.

"No reason," Suzie said. "I'm just scared, is all. Jumpy. Spooky. Some people are that way. I can't help it."

"It's okay," I said.

We walked down the road like that, holding hands, walking slowly in the dusk. It was about three miles down the gravel road to my cabin. Suzie knew the way. We heard owls as we walked along the river and saw lots of deer. Once, for no reason, I turned and looked back, but I saw nothing, saw no one.

If Randy can have such white-hot passion for a thing—bowhunting—he can, I understand full well, have just as much heat in his hate. It spooks me the way he doesn't bring Suzie presents anymore in the old, hopeful way. The flat looks he gives me could mean anything: they rattle me.

It's like I can't *see* him.

Sometimes I'm afraid to go into the woods.

But I do anyway. I go hunting in the fall and cut wood in the fall and winter, fish in the spring, and go for walks in the summer, walks and drives up to the tops of the high snowy mountains—and there are times when I feel someone or something is just behind me, following at a distance, and I'll turn around, frightened and angry both, and I won't see anything, but still, later on into the walk, I'll feel it again.

But I feel other things, too: I feel my happiness with Suzie. I feel the sun on my face and on my shoulders. I like the way we sit on the porch again, the way we used to, with drinks in hand, and watch the end of day, watch the deer come slipping down into the river.

I'm frightened, but it feels delicious.

This year at the Halloween party, it dumped on us; it began snowing the day before and continued on through the night and all through Halloween day and then Halloween night, snowing harder than ever. The roof over the saloon groaned that night under the load of new snow, but we had the party anyway and kept dancing, all of us leaping around and waltzing, drinking, proposing toasts, and arm-wrestling, then leaping up again and dancing some more, with all the antlers from all the animals in the valley strapped to our heads—everyone. It look pagan. We all whooped and danced. Davey and Suzie danced in each other's arms, swirled and pirouetted; she was so light and so free, and I watched them and grinned. Randy sat on the porch and drank beers and watched, too, and smiled. It was a polite smile.

All of the rest of us drank and stomped around. We shook our heads at each other and pretended we were deer, pretended we were elk.

We ran out of beer around three in the morning, and we all started gathering up our skis, rounding up rides, people with trucks who could take us home. The rumble of trucks being warmed up began, and the beams of headlights crisscrossed the road in all directions, showing us just how hard it really was snowing. The flakes were as large as the biggest goose feathers. Because Randy and I lived up the same road, Davey drove us home, and Suzie took hold of the tow rope and skied with us.

Davey drove slowly because it was hard to see the road in such a storm.

Suzie had had a lot to drink—we all had—and she held on to the rope with both hands, her deer antlers slightly askew, and she began to ask Randy some questions about his hunting—not razzing him, as I thought she would, but simply questioning him—things she'd been wondering for a long time, I supposed, but had been too angry to ask. We watched the brake lights in front of us, watched the snow spiraling into our faces and concentrated on holding on to the rope. As usual, we all seemed to have forgotten the antlers that were on our heads.

"What's it like?" Suzie kept wanting to know. "I mean, what's it *really* like?"

We were sliding through the night, holding on to the rope, being pulled through the night. The snow was striking our faces, caking our eyebrows, and it was so cold that it was hard to speak.

"You're a real asshole, you know?" Suzie said, when Randy wouldn't answer. "You're too cold-blooded for me," she said. "You scare me, mister."

Randy just stared straight ahead, his face hard and flat and blank, and he held on to the rope.

I'd had way too much to drink. We all had. We slid over some rough spots in the road.

"Suzie, honey," I started to say—I have no idea what I was going to say after that—something to defend Randy, I think—but then I stopped, because Randy turned and looked at me, for just a second, with fury, terrible fury, which I could *feel* as well as see, even in my drunkenness. But then the mask, the polite mask, came back down over him, and we continued down the road in silence, the antlers on our heads bobbing and weaving, a fine target for anyone who might not have understood that we weren't wild animals.

LEE MERRILL BYRD

Major Six Pockets

Tennessee sprang out the car door the minute John turned the handle, barking across the low rainy meadow at the four steaming cows; they lumbered down towards the stream, their leader—the biggest one—turning suddenly, clumsily, pawing the ground.

Daddy! shrieked Andy. They're going to kill Tennessee. But no, said Daddy, it was not true. That cow who pawed the ground was a woman, Daddy said—can't you see her tits hanging down?—and women cows are hopeless in the face of a dog like Tennessee.

Now, if that was a bull, said Daddy, raising his eyebrows. Um um um . . .

Yes, said Andy, raising what little eyebrows remained to him, if that was a bull. Um um um . . .

John hung out the car door, marking the landscape like a

tour guide, while Daddy bumped the Mazda down into place beside a pile of branches. Here, said John, is the firewood. And here is a bush. Yes, here is where we park. There is the water.

Daddy said, Here it is, the perfect camping spot. Just like I told you from the beginning. We got out of the car and stood looking up at the soft gray clouds that huddled at the mouth of the canyon. Susie got out and stood beside Daddy, and John and Andy came and fell in place. They looked things over, the indolent sky, the steep mountains, the flat meadow skirted with chokecherry bushes, the pile of branches, the white rocks already set for a campfire. Up above, a long distance off, a last lone car rumbled on through the San Juans.

Here it is, said Andy. The perfect camping spot.

Here is where it began, with Tennessee and the imitation bull and with the finding of this spot, the perfect camping spot, as Daddy called it. Here is where it began, the vacating, the vacation, here on the low secret meadow, hidden in a pocket of the ragged mountains.

But it had started for Daddy a long time before that, the talking about it, the working out of it. It had started for Daddy almost from the beginning, before we knew about Andy, which way he would go, before he lost the ear and his hair and then the fingers on his left hand; long before it became apparent about John and his face. It had started for Daddy almost from the beginning, when Andy lay on a high bed, in isolation, wrapped in white gauze, and did not talk. Daddy would talk to him, would talk to him about it, about the trip we would take, about the vacation, about the mountains and the perfect camping spot. Daddy said they would catch fish, they would catch rainbow trout, they would catch browns and cutthroats, they would use flies and worms and salmon eggs, garlic-flavored marshmallows and grasshoppers, and they would take the fish and Mother would cook them over the campfire in a pan filled with butter. Daddy said they would ask Susie to fry potatoes, too, and there would be Cokes and Jewish pickles and later some dessert.

One day in March after a long night and a high fever, Andy in a thin and broken whisper said he wanted pie. Cherry pie. The nurse said they didn't have any. Daddy's voice began to shake. He told her it didn't matter, that Andy didn't want the cherry pie now, he wanted the cherry pie for later, for after the fish. Wasn't that right? Daddy asked Andy and Andy shut his eyes and nodded solemnly.

Daddy, when he went to visit John on the ward, told John all about the plans he and Andy had been making. Daddy said he'd talked to Andy about where Eskimos lived, and that Andy seemed to agree that that might be the perfect place for a camping trip. Did John know that there in that place where Eskimos lived everyone slept together naked under a mound of caribou furs and there were lots of girls and all the girls liked to dance?

John listened intently, chewing on the bandages that covered his hands. He did not think that he wanted to camp in a place like that. He would rather camp in a place that was just so-so where if there were any girls they didn't dance and if you slept under caribou furs you could wear your pajamas.

Daddy talked to Ronnie Tate in the bed next to John's and wondered what kind of son he had who did not like girls who danced. He asked Carnell Hughes on the other side of the room what he thought about sleeping naked and the three young boys giggled and waited for Daddy to come back. When he did he sat on a chair in the middle of the room and brought news of Andy and the latest plans.

On the first of April, they took Andy out of isolation and put him in the big room with John and with Ronnie Tate and with Carnell Hughes. Andy looked at John and said, His skin, and John said in his most matter-of-fact way, He's bald. Daddy laughed until he cried and began to sing, Christmas is a-coming, the geese are getting fat, and clapped his hands until John wailed, Oh Daddy, stop.

That same day after lunch Daddy went to Colonel Bubbie's Army-Navy Surplus and bought a pair of shorts, Italian six-pockets, and filled the pockets with stuff for the trip: a pocket knife, some fish hooks and salmon eggs, fishing line and candy bars, and they spent the afternoon eating Milky Ways and looking over Daddy's Italian six-pockets and talking about Alaska and the Ozarks and New Mexico, about the Rockies and the Blue Hills and other perfect camping spots.

But April was no better. Andy's blood was full of infection. The antibiotic they gave him to cure it made him throw up and he could not talk. The tub men came to get him in the mornings, to scrub the dead skin away from the burns, and Andy screamed and Daddy walked the halls. He wasn't sure where we would go anymore and he agreed with John, that a so-so place would be just as good as a place where Eskimos lived.

The doctors said they needed to operate on Andy again and that John had a staph infection in the graft on his cheek and must have more IVs. Ronnie Tate said would Daddy tell them again about the Eskimos and the dancing girls but Daddy said he'd have to wait, he did not want to talk about the trip anymore for a little while.

In the evening two days after Andy's surgery, Daddy and the nurse lifted Andy onto a chair and the nurse said that Andy would have to sit there awhile for a change and Andy cried and cried and said he hurt and the nurse finally asked Daddy to step out in the hall. Later, Daddy and the nurse put Andy back in bed, one under his head, one holding his feet, there being no place in between that they could touch, and they covered him with a sheet and tucked it in and Andy began to talk and did not stop. He said to John that he was sorry about John's corduroy coat, that he had worn John's corduroy coat that day and that it had gotten burned and did Daddy know where the corduroy coat was or his blue pants, the ones he had worn while they played in the fort and had he lost his sneakers too, the new ones, and did John remember how Morgan had thrown dirt on him to make the fire go out and did John remember the ice cream man who called the fire engine and did Mom know how to cook fish and that after the fish they would have cherry pie. He shook all over, he talked so fast and he said that he liked the Italian six-pockets and he called Daddy Major Six Pockets and Daddy sat down and could not talk.

Then the plans began in earnest. And every day they discussed another place. There were the Chiricahuas and the Sangre de Cristos, the Smokies in Tennessee where Daddy was born, the Mississippi and the Shenandoah. There was Missoula and Butte and Chaco Canyon and Mesa Verde and Cheyenne and the Florida Keys and the Yucatan and the Black Hills.

But—much later, when the boys were home again—Susie said she just wanted to go to Colorado, because, after all, that was where she was born; and according to the things that she had heard about Colorado from Daddy, there was a cottage there in a big meadow, a little honeymoon cottage where she had once lived and surrounding that cottage were hills and mountains where elk and deer roamed, snakes and mountain lions and coyotes. And in the meadow bulls moaned and pranced and down around all of it came crashing the mighty Rio Grande. She was a true Colorado girl and needed to go back. As proof, she reminded the boys that when she was hardly a day old, she had played naked in ten or more feet of snow. Hadn't Daddy said so?

And so the vacation was to Colorado, to Susie's ancestral homeland because, Daddy said, Susie is the oldest and even though we won't get to go where the boys wanted to go, all the things that they had dreamed about and talked about while they were in the hospital were right there in Colorado: cherry pies and caribou furs and dancing girls and sleeping bags and perfect camping spots. And anyway, Daddy said, it would have to be Susie's trip because the fire had been the boys'.

*   *   *

19

Andy took Dr. Phineas, the green frog, and Smudge, the stuffed bear. Also, he needed a backpack. He filled its pockets and corners with erasers and magnets, some photos he had gotten from Grandma, pennies, crayons, and a ruler. Dr. Phineas nearly fell out, even with Smudge crammed in beside him, so it seemed necessary to bring a second brown bear to make the fit complete.

John had books, many more than one, because of Andy and all the things that Andy had in his backpack. And John brought tapes and what were tapes without the tape recorder?

Daddy helped Susie hide her violin between the cooler and the back seat beneath two sleeping bags. She put a shoe box containing her diaries and some pesos and soap and a small tea set and a something she was crocheting under the front seat and stuffed her jacket in behind it.

Daddy brought books and a pad of paper to write on in case of a poem. There was mayonnaise and peanut butter and salami and crackers and instant coffee, plenty of bacon, sacks of oranges and apples, a pineapple from Mexico, and some sugarless chewing gum. There was a hatchet and a shovel and two delicate fishing rods jammed in between the seats and the doors. The trunk strapped to the roof held a change of clothes for every person for every eventuality, but for the most part, it was full of pressure garments for the boys and splints and ace wraps and gauze and adhesive tape.

Well, said Daddy. None of this takes up much room.

Susie sat in the front seat and talked. She said that Texas was all right. Though it was hot. Though of course El Paso was not as hot as the rest of Texas. El Paso was not really at all like any other part of Texas. In the first place there were no Texans in El Paso. In the second place there was Juarez and all of that. Daddy listened and dreamed and Susie talked intently. John snoozed, his left eye partly open even while he slept, and Andy colored, Dr. Phineas looking on. Tennessee turned and sighed between the cooler and the violin and the five extra pairs of shoes.

Daddy drove on up through Hatch and Truth or Consequences, on past Albuquerque and Santa Fe and Española, all
in one day, driving towards Colorado and the perfect camping
spot. Why did you and Mom ever leave Colorado in the first
place? asked Susie. I mean, if you worked for Texas millionaires
and ate venison and had the honeymoon cottage all to yourselves and the Rio Grande in your back yard?

John and Andy leaned forward to listen. Your mother and
I, said Daddy, had things to do.

Yeah? said Susie. Like what?

Your mother and I had work cut out for us in the big city.
We couldn't work for Texas millionaires forever. It was too
easy.

Anyway, he went on, we were warned in a dream that John
would arrive any minute and that he intended to be born in Albuquerque, in a little rent house in Albuquerque where the
landlord next door was always drunk, so we had to quick hus-
tle and pack up and move down the Rio Grande.

Oh, Daddy . . .

Tres Piedras had a cafe and a grocery and two gas stations.

Well, said Daddy, there was a second dream. It said, Leave
any minute for Las Cruces for Andy intends to come howling
and screaming forth from his mother's belly at exactly five in
the morning on the twenty-fifth day . . .

Andy sang to himself all across the high plain between
Tres Piedras and Antonito, hanging his good arm out the
window.

John peered into the tape recorder listening to the Lone
Ranger talk things over with Tonto. The Cavendish gang had
just killed the Lone Ranger's brother and all his friends. Those
evil men knew the Lone Ranger by sight. If they know that one
man escaped their ambush, worried the Lone Ranger, they'll
look for him and kill him.

Them not know one man escape, said Tonto. Tonto bury
five men, make six graves. Crook think you die with others.

Good, wheezed the Lone Ranger. Then my name shall be buried forever with my brother and my friends. From now on my face must be concealed. A disguise, perhaps, he considered. Or maybe a mask. That's it! A mask . . .

Daddy wore his Italian six-pockets: two pockets on the side, two pockets in the front, two pockets behind, with four buttons up the fly that he never managed to button all at once. John and Andy wore their masks, brown elastic hoods that held white life masks in place. Susie wore a straw hat and people stared. Daddy stopped in Albuquerque for gas and people stared. We stopped in Ojo Caliente for lunch and took the boys' masks off so they could eat and everyone in the restaurant grew quiet and tried to pretend they didn't notice. In Antonito we stopped to buy flies and hooks and everybody watched while Daddy discussed salmon eggs loudly and deliberately with his children, Andy breathing hard and fast from the pressure of the mask on his nose, John, solemn and intent, just his eyes, his lips.

From Antonito on, Daddy drove hard, pushing on into the mountains, looking for that conjunction of the perfect camping spot and the setting sun.

The road from Antonito towards Platoro was all dirt and rocks and Daddy drove it fast, the Mazda eclipsed by the rising dust. Tennessee stood up, his nose pressed against the window, swaying as Daddy took the curves. Susie said how late it was, and John said that Daddy drove too fast. After a few miles there was a sign, a tent pitched upon solid rock, and behind the sign among the trees a neat circle of cars and RVs just settling down for some outdoor adventure and Susie said, There it is, Daddy, there's the perfect camping spot, but Daddy only drove faster, on past more signs with pitched tents, drawing up toward the edge of the wrong side of the road from time to time to peer down through thick forest, over sheer cliffs. We're getting closer, he said, as eager as Tennessee.

The forest opened up into meadow that rolled away from the road toward the hills. Daddy slowed to look, sticking his head out the window, talking it over. There's a stream. Too close to the road. What do you think?

But nothing seemed quite right and Daddy drove on.

There is no perfect camping spot, said Susie. It will be dark and we'll be lost and it will be cold and it will rain.

Daddy turned off the road, to the left, down a rutted path that crossed a little bridge and went up on top of a hill. Let's look around, he said.

Andy and John and Daddy got out and stood looking through the trees at the flat green meadow below. They walked down some and the three of them peed while Susie sat in the front seat and watched until they disappeared and watched the same spot until they came back again. They got in the car.

Well, Sus, said Daddy, I think we've found it.

The road down from the hill to the perfect camping spot was pitted with animal holes and big hidden rocks and at one point was so slanted that the Mazda felt as if it would tip over. The last curve revealed the meadow, empty and waiting.

The sun began its long summer descent at one end of the slender canyon while the ragged clouds pushed for entrance at the other; down in between, in the long flat meadow, our camp took its shape: tent and Mazda, firewood, cooler, trunk, sleeping bags. Daddy built a fire for the supper and said he thought he might try to fish while he waited for the fire to make coals. The kids each declared that they would go first, until Daddy said that for tonight, since it was almost dark, he was the only one who could fish. But that they could watch. And if they were good maybe they could each hold the pole once. Maybe twice. And that though they would bring the second pole, they probably wouldn't use it since fly fishing was an art that had to be taught and it was getting too dark to do any teaching.

They walked up the meadow, carrying the two poles, looking for a pool of water in the stream where trouts and browns
and cutthroats would be congregating. Tennessee made wide
circles around them, Daddy in his six-pockets and sneakers,
Susie in her straw hat, the boys masked and splinted. Just as the
sun hit the edge of the mountain, they were back, unmasked
and unsplinted, shoes and shorts and six-pockets soaking.
Daddy said here was proof that every camping trip required an
extra set of shoes and they all changed and stood around the
campfire while Daddy told them again about his backpacking
trip through the Waminuches with Uncle Steve and how Uncle
Steve and he had been caught in a driving rain and had to quick
set up their tent and how he had had to rub Uncle Steve's
hands and feet because Uncle Steve was shaking so hard from
the cold. But how that was the price a person had to pay when
he went camping with skinny people.

After supper Daddy said, Let's get up early and go fishing
first thing. The kids got into the tent and laughed and argued
for a long time, about whose head should be where, and about
who would have Tennessee sleeping next to him, and about
how loud John snored with his mask on. Daddy roamed
around the campfire, getting things ready for the morning,
looking up at the sky from time to time. He had a cigarette and
some tequila and sat on a log, staring into the fire, listening to
the kids talk. Much later, when they had finally fallen asleep, he
covered the coals with dirt and made a bed on the ground near
the door of the tent, but the minute he got in his bag it started
to rain, so he came up into the Mazda, where the back seat was
pulled down.

Think you're smart, do you? he said, making room for
himself. We slept the way you sleep the first night on camping
trips, just so-so, sometimes resting so deep inside the sound of
the rain, sometimes sore, turning and turning to find just the
right position. Then just before dawn, he woke up suddenly
and said, I think the kids are having fun, don't you? and

went back to sleep as if that was that: the very last thing on his mind.

That first morning he taught them to fish. They went back to the deep pool up the meadow before breakfast. He showed them how to cast, how to let the attractive, glittering flies float along the water as if they were alive, how to turn the reel quickly and strike again to catch the attention of those trouts and browns and cutthroats who lay waiting fat and sleek to take the bait. The flies caught on every rock and bush and Andy when they came back described the way in which Major Six Pockets had waded in and out of the deep pool to recover the line and how they hadn't caught anything this time because Tennessee had been leaping up and down the stream and barking after cows and scaring the fish and how Susie and John had taken much more than their share of turns. When Susie wasn't listening, Daddy said she fly fished as if she'd been casting in the womb.

For breakfast there were eggs cooked in plenty of bacon grease, the sun coming up sly and warm along the mouth of the canyon. Afterward, Daddy boiled water over the fire and took it and Andy to the stream to bathe. From a distance Andy looked like he wore a coat of armor across his chest and back, the skin was so scarred there and still so furious and red and it drew down tight against the soft whiteness of his stomach. Daddy washed him all over with warm water and then made him lie down quick to rinse off. He said how Andy was the only boy he knew who had only seven fingers but ten belly buttons and together they traced the convolutions that erupted on the upper part of his body. Andy said that John and Susie had to take a bath too but Daddy said no, that Susie being not burned could bathe every three or four days the way you did on camping trips and that John having no more open spots on his body could wait until tomorrow. Andy fussed and cried and said it was not fair, that just because he was burned he had to bathe every day. Daddy carried him to the Mazda and laid him down so he could pick the dead skin away from the open spots. Andy studied the slow movement of the sterile tweezers in Daddy's hand while Daddy strained and squinted to avoid the raw skin and Andy's screams, and rubbed cream on him, ranging slowly and methodically over that small eroded chest with his finger-tips, massaging the withered arm with his whole hand, and wrapped both with ace wraps and put the pressure garments and the splints and the mask back on. Tennessee licked the bacon grease out of the fry pan and Daddy said that he would like to try fishing on the other part of the stream. Susie and John grabbed the poles. Let your mother go first, said Daddy. Susie came next, pressing close, then John, then Daddy and Andy with Tennessee behind and in front and behind again, announcing himself to the trout and browns and cutthroats who waited fat and sleek in the deep pools at the top of the meadow.

The stream crossed the meadow east not a hundred yards from the perfect camping spot. There was a little trail there on the other side but Andy said he could not walk, that his shoes were so wet from walking across the stream with them on and that Daddy would have to carry him. He cried and fell down in a heap insisting that he could not keep going, that his squeaking shoes hurt his feet, and Daddy stopped, not sure whether to go on or to go back. Susie said that Andrew was a baby and John said that it was nothing to walk in wet shoes and Andy wailed. We walked on ahead, Susie and John looking back every little bit to watch Daddy kneeling beside Andy, taking his shoes and socks off and squeezing the water out; they could see Daddy talking to Andy and trying to shut him up. Susie called back for them to hurry up and Daddy told her just to go on and mind her own business. Susie yelled to Andy that her shoes were already dry and Daddy said to shut up, just shut up, so we went on, up where the chokecherries got thicker and the trees were taller and the sun not quite so bright to hurt the boys' skin.

After a while Daddy came up with Andy behind him sulk-ing. One of the fishing lines was all tangled up and Daddy sat cross-legged on the ground trying to straighten it while Susie demonstrated the art of casting to her brothers. She stood on a big rock and repeated all of Daddy's instructions on fly fishing as if they were her own and John and Andy watched her, caught by the volume of what she knew, mesmerized by each toss into the glimmering pool. Daddy looked up and looking, was arrested by the sight of the children: Susie, high on the rock, in her eleventh year suddenly so tall and beautiful; John, his face turned up to listen to her, that face that no amount of studying could change, the one side ravaged by fire, the other side handsome, perfect; Andy, at the age of six, bald, without an ear, with only seven fingers. Daddy looked. They played, mindless of him, mindless of themselves, laughing. And the line lay tangled across his knees.

We fished there an hour, then walked on up the canyon, up a trail toward the steep mountains, climbing until Andy's com-plaints were unbearable, and then found a place to sit while Daddy took out the map. He traced the road between An-tonito and Platoro with his finger and located the perfect camping spot somewhere in between. Susie said if we drove far-ther up we would find Blowout Pass and Cornwall's Nose and John said, Look, here is Elephant Mountain and Handkerchief Mesa and Andy because he could not read screamed until he could squeeze in close to Daddy and touch the map himself. Daddy took Andy's finger and led it all over the local terrain until it fell with a thud into Lost Lake.

Then Daddy lit a cigarette and pointed to the mountains in front of him, mountains that erupted from the earth, pocked with sinuous ridges and red the color of dirt, and said those were called the Pinnacles and John wanted to know why and how come they were the way they were. Daddy looked at John awhile and didn't answer, as if he hadn't heard, so John asked again and Daddy said abruptly they were called the Pinnacles because they went straight up and were like towers and that the Pinnacles and all the mountains around, the whole range of the San Juans, were formed by fire.

They fished all that afternoon, before and after supper, but it wasn't until the next day, until they began to act as if they'd been in that canyon all their lives, that anything was caught. It was just before supper and they had gone again to that deep pool where they had gone the first time; and John came back across the meadow alone, his hands behind him and grinning, with the fish and the story. It was Susie's fish, he said, and her line had been so tight and she screamed, Daddy, it's a fish, but Daddy had gotten mad and said he was tired of wading out into the pool to untangle their lines and that people were go-ing to either have to learn to cast or learn to wade. Susie screamed and screamed and Andy and John screamed and screamed, trying to persuade Daddy that this was no false alarm, but Daddy said it was a rock and that this was the last time, that in nothing less than two days he had nearly ruined his sneakers.

John said, Daddy waded out and put his hand down to get the line and when he brought it up, there it was, the fish, and Daddy laughed and slapped the water and Susie said, See Daddy. See Daddy, and Daddy sent John back to spread the news. Come on, Mom, he said and we walked back across the meadow to hear the story again, once from Daddy and once from Susie and once more from Andy. We stayed there by the pool until they could barely see, until two more fish were caught, and then came back to the perfect camping spot and ate them, cooked over the campfire in a pan filled with butter, each bite causing Daddy to tell the story again, until Susie's first catch had settled forever in the memories of the children, until just the smell of fish or the sight of the moon or the feel of mountain air on their bodies would remind them again all through their lives of their Daddy and the trip he took them on into the mountains that first year after the fire.

That night the kids went to bed early, right after they ate, because they wanted to get up first thing and catch another fish. Tennessee crawled in the tent beside them, exhausted. Daddy wanted to talk. He sat beside the fire. He said he wondered did every parent think that only his own kids were remarkable? He smoothed a pattern into the dirt with his shoe, going over and over it until it was a perfect little fan shape, edged on both sides. Don't you think the kids are remarkable? he said. He could not believe how the fire had changed them all, he could not believe how happy they always were. It was what he would have wanted them to be, but never just by telling them could have made them that way. Do you see what I mean? he asked. It was like the fire itself had given them what we never could have.

He leaned forward, his elbows on his knees, and took a piece of his hair and twisted it around and around his finger, staring off to where the mountains lay like paper silhouettes against the sky. After a while he said, Don't you think John's face is getting better? Don't you think that eye is not pulling down quite so much?

They fished all that week, most often in the deep pool just down below the perfect camping spot, but sometimes up the meadow; once Daddy even got everybody in the car and went on up the road as if he were going to Platoro. He stopped at Saddle Creek, a wide stream that wound like a snake through a damp high grassed plain. It was flat there and the wind blew.

There was a man at Saddle Creek. He came walking up the stream wearing high rubber boots with his pole in his hand and his fish basket across his shoulder, walking slow, his eyes on the water. He was the first person we had seen since the vacation began and Daddy when he saw him got excited and said so quickly, Say, how's the fishing? The man looked up and blinked at Daddy and then past Daddy and past Susie at John and Andy and no further. Andy had his splint off and John wore his mask. The man stopped and blinked again; and Daddy remembering moved back some and directly in front of Andy. How's the fishing? Daddy said again.

The man had been drinking. It was noon and he smelled like cheap wine. He didn't move. What do you have there? he said to Daddy. Daddy's face got tight. Behind your back? said the man. Daddy said, It's my family. The man opened his mouth so slow and looked as if he was going to fall forward; he sneezed suddenly and took an old handkerchief out of his pocket to wipe his nose.

Yeah? he said. He stared at Daddy. They're my sons, said Daddy. He brought Andy forward, his hand on Andy's shoulder.

Hey, Sonny, said the man real slow. He looked at Andy for a long time, squinting, going from the bald spot to the ear to his arm. What happened to your hand? he said finally.

Andy looked down at the water. He was in a fire, said Daddy.

Playing with matches? said the man. The sun by then held at the center of the canyon, directly overhead.

No, said Daddy. The color drained down from his temples.

The man looked over at John. It was another boy who had matches, said Daddy quickly, it was an accident, these boys don't play with matches.

Yeah? said the man. He dropped his pole, an expensive bamboo one, and his fancy fish basket into the stream and began to try to get something out of his back pocket. Daddy bent over to get the basket and the pole out of the water, but the man flapped his hand at him to let him know it didn't matter. Finding nothing in his pocket he rubbed himself all over the front of his shirt, but seemed to forget for a while what he was after. I'd have killed my kids if I found them playing with

30

matches, he said, his hands poised over his belly. He began searching again.

He found what he was looking for in the pocket of his pants: a roll of money. He thumbed through the bills, lots of twenties and tens, deliberating, then tugged at one, releasing it, and leaned over, nearly falling, to stick it in Andy's hand. You better find some other friends, little buddy, he said. He stood up and looked at Daddy out of one eye. What did you do to that kid? he asked. Did you kill him?

Well, said Daddy. He searched along the meadow past the man's head, biting at his upper lip. That boy is our friend, said Daddy quietly. He's one of the boys' good friends. And then a frantic burst of enthusiasm: How long you been up here? Have you caught anything? Where are you from?

Yeah? said the man. He sneezed again, wiping his mouth off with the back of his hand, and began to re-consider his money.

Have you caught anything? Daddy said again, a little louder, but the man seemed intent on the roll of bills. Listen, said Daddy, his eye on the money too, these kids don't need money. He took hold of Andy's arm, trying to push him on up out of the stream.

Sure they do, the man went right on counting. Kid can always use a little money. Can't you, buddy? he said looking over at John. Here, he said. He breathed out of his mouth, short and hard. Here's something to buy some candy with. It was a twenty dollar bill. What's the matter, buddy? You can't use a little money? John looked over at Daddy and then at the money Andy had clutched in his hand. He came forward looking down at the stream. The man held the bill out but wouldn't let go of it.

Say, tell me something, pal, said the man, what's this thing you've got covering your face?

These kids don't need money, said Daddy. Come on, John let's go, we have to go on.

Whoa, now, pardner, said the man. Don't get yourself all worked up. I'm just asking, just curious. Just wanting to know what happened to these poor little fellers. You don't always act like this when people try to do something nice for your kids, do you?

Look, said Daddy, slowly and deliberately, my boy is wearing a mask. He has to wear a mask because he was burned on his face, and burned skin will scar unless you keep pressure on it to keep it flat.

Yeah? said the man. He studied the twenty dollar bill he held in his hand. Well, you know what I always say, said the man, putting the bill back into the roll of money. I always say that nothing is so bad you got to hide it.

Look! exploded Daddy. He's not hiding anything. He has to keep it on. Daddy pushed on John's arm to make him go on, up out of the stream, and looked back at Susie to get her to come follow, but her eye, like John's, was caught by the roll of bills.

What about the girl? said the man, suddenly aware of her. Girl could use a little money, too, couldn't she? Couldn't you, honey? The thumbing through the money began again, that process now at the very center of the canyon, the man studying each shift of his finger, droning on about matches and fires and the way he raised his own kids to be decent, while Daddy, grabbing and pushing, severed Susie and John from the sight and the sound of him, striding out ahead across the high plain toward the car, dragging Andy by the hand.

Daddy had said he would take the kids to Platoro after they fished, to the store in Platoro so they could get some candy, but he turned instead and drove back along the edge of the canyon towards the campsite. He stopped the car finally just short of the pile of firewood, but nobody moved. He stared out over the flat meadow, chewing on his lip, then looked back as if to talk but didn't say anything. Andy still held his treasure tight in his hand where the man had stuck it. Daddy studied it.

How much did he give you? said Daddy. Andy opened his hand but would not look up. Twenty dollars, said Daddy. I want you to share that with your brother and sister, hear? he said and turned back, straight in his seat.

It was hot and no one moved. Finally Daddy said, He was drunk. And said again, after a while, Your mother and I are real proud of you kids. You know that? He turned to look at the three of them. Don't be afraid when people stare, he said, when they ask questions. Just be polite, just do the best you can. He looked down at his hands, empty before him, and then back up at the kids. OK? he said.

We didn't do much the rest of that day, a little fishing, a little gathering of firewood, some half-hearted naps. For supper there were ranchstyle beans and bacon and tortillas. Nobody mentioned the cherry pie that Daddy had planned to buy in Platoro. Daddy and John and Andy stood around the campfire with their hands in their pockets while Susie drew jagged lines in the dirt with a twig.

Whoa, now, pardner, said Daddy suddenly, in a deep slow drawl. The three of them looked over at him. Whoa, now pardner, Daddy drawled again, why ya'll don't always act like this, do you?

Why, no, pardner, said Susie, standing up, brushing herself off. Whenever we see that much money we always act just like this. She froze with her eyes popping out of her head and her mouth wide open. John blinked in amazement. Yeah, he said, just like this, imitating his big sister. Daddy let his jaw drop, too.

Did you see how much money he had, Daddy? shrieked Andy, running over to tug on Daddy and get his attention.

Did I see how much money he had? said Daddy. He flopped down suddenly on the ground and lay like a dead man, with his eyes and mouth gaping open, even the rigors of death unable to erase the astonishment he felt at the drunk man's wealth.

Daddy, Daddy, Daddy, John sputtered, did you see it? Tens and tens and tens and tens and twenties.

I saw a fifty dollar bill, said Susie.

Daddy, said Andy, what if he had given me a fifty dollar bill?

Daddy sat up. He leered at Andy and said, Here you go, little buddy—plunking a rock down in Andy's hand—but you better find yourself a new daddy.

Yeah, said Susie, and while you're at it, pal, get rid of your mother.

And your brother and sister, too, said John.

Move to a new city, pard, said Susie.

Daddy stood up and went outside the circle of the camp-fire where they couldn't see him and came back inside, stumbling along with his eyes down on the ground and aiming straight for Andy. He rammed right into him and fell back, startled, whining, Why . . . Why . . . what happened to your hand, buddy?

His hand! said Susie, and grabbed Andy and turned him around, pointing to his head: This kid is bald.

Yeah, said John, did you notice that this kid is bald?

Why . . . did something happen to your head, little pal? moaned Daddy.

It went on like that for a long time, Daddy playing the drunk man, weaving in and out of the circle, the innocent and guileless cowpoke lurching smack up against that disconcerting vision of Daddy—played by John—in his half-buttoned six-pockets and Susie in her straw hat, of the real John in his mask and Andy without his splint; the wad of money coming in and out of his pocket, dropping from time to time all over the ground, being doled out according to the more or less pitiful merits of the one upon whom he had stumbled, his generosity spun out by Daddy before their eyes so they could squander and spend.

It was nine or past before they could be got into the tent, still talking and laughing and John almost beside himself with the ramifications of the drunk man's eyeful. Susie, Susie, Susie, he kept saying to get her attention, bursting with some new aspect of the case, and it was his voice that we listened to as we sat beside the fire, that stalwart, practical, ancient voice trying to drown out Susie and Andy, suddenly as talkative and confessional as he had been heard but once or twice in his short lifetime.

The moon made its way along the top of the canyon while the three of them talked; we listened, not moving for fear of losing the opportunity. They talked it all through that night, the whole thing, about the party, about Susie's tenth birthday party and how Susie in purple stood at the top of the front steps and waved the boys goodbye as they went to stay at Morgan's house; about how—did Susie remember?—John sat in the back seat with Morgan and had a plate of party cupcakes on his lap. The fort in Morgan's yard had been built the week before of palm branches and an old Christmas tree and John said there were voices in the alley, voices and girls laughing and then the smell of smoke and suddenly the whole thing went up in flames and Morgan ran out and then back and John was stuck on a branch and pulled away and then Andy could not get out, could not get out, and Morgan pulled him out covered with flames.

And threw dirt on him, Susie said. And began to tell it her way. Susie, Susie, Susie, said John, until she shut up.

Listen, he said, it started spreading around. I felt real scared. I felt like I was going to die, except that Morgan found a way for us to get out. So when Andy got out there was fire on his clothes and I felt real scared.

You were stuck inside, said Susie, matter-of-factly.

Listen, Susie, said John, I was already out and I'll tell you what it was like. The easiest part in the whole thing to go through was getting out. And he went on from there, his story: about the plane ride down to Galveston and his eyes and his mouth swollen shut, about Johnson and Jackson in the tub room and how they told jokes and how they always let him watch the TV when they scrubbed him, about the surgeries and the shots and the doctors in their white coats standing in crowds around his bed talking about his face and how they could fix it. And all this time thinking it was the girls laughing in the alley who had thrown a match, just like Morgan told his mother, until Morgan flew down to Galveston and told them how he had seen a book of matches—did they remember?— just before he had come into the fort for the last time and he had struck one and thrown it aside, thinking it was out, and that he hadn't meant to do it and that he was sorry.

Well, Susie wanted to know, what did you tell him, what did you say?

And Johnny said, I said, Sure, OK. But did Susie remember about the time when she had been there when he was finally out of the hospital and they were just waiting for Andy to heal up so they could go home and they all went to the bookstore on the Strand and bought comic books?

Daddy stood up. Um, he sighed and chewed his lip and sat down again for lack of anything else to do while John went on, on and on, remembering only moments of pleasure: the comic books and the Strand and the funny old stores and how Daddy had stood in the middle of the room one night and read *Alice in Wonderland* to him and Andy and Ronnie Tate and Carnell Hughes. His voice pressed forward steadily, cheerfully from the tent; up above the moon crossed the Pinnacles and then suddenly there was a story we had never heard before, he had never talked about. The first week of school—did Susie remember the first week of school when they finally got back home?— when John had to wear his mask all during school?

Yeah, what about it? Susie wanted to know.

Well, said John, did she know the big boy with the black hair in his class, the one that he had invited to his sixth birthday party whose name he couldn't remember?

Oh yeah, said Susie, that one.

Well, said John, that boy, whatever his name is, made a bunch of the kids who could not speak English take stones and throw them at me.

Oh yeah, Susie said. Did it hurt?

But that was the last Daddy heard, the last thing he listened to. He stood up then and walked away, on up the meadow, as far from the sounds of their voices as he could get.

Daddy brought the Mazda up away from the perfect camping spot exactly one week after he had brought it down and went on a half-day's bumpy ride to descend into the San Luis Valley, there at South Fork where Susie was born, and spent the next hour sightseeing. Here, he said, is the honeymoon cottage and there beside it the road up into the mountains where Mother carried Susie on her back each afternoon, and there the bushes full of rosehips that Mother made into a syrup to feed Susie when she got sick. And there! the bulls that she stood at the window ledge and stared at, the moaning prancing bulls; and o Lord! two buffalo! but of course—every Texas millionaire had a buffalo or two amongst their longhorns. And see! the Rio Grande, crashing around in the back yard, just like I said, Daddy said.

But they hardly listened. Andy fell asleep while Daddy toured the countryside and Johnny read and even Susie after a while was not so interested, ancestral territory or not, and turned down Daddy's offer to drive her by the hospital where she was born. She began to talk about school, about getting ready for school, about notebook paper and pencils and a ring binder and whether or not she would get Mr. Lafarelle for homeroom again. Daddy drove down through Del Norte and on through Monte Vista while she and John made lists of school items and the absolute minimum of clothes that would get them through: 2 pr. jeans, 2 pr. socks, one sneakers, shorts for P.E. The Mazda entered Alamosa and from there passed south, back toward Antonito; the flat plains of Manassa, the quaint stores, even the deep silences of the Sangre de Cristos and the San Juans unnoticed. They were already home. There was school and Sarah and Greg and Jeannie and Junior and John Maxfield and the cat to get back to and it appeared that the trip was over though they still had miles to go.

DIANE DeSANDERS

When He Saw Me

The thing I really want to tell you about is my father and the way he was always on the run on those feet, but the thing is that I don't know what to do with him once I get him on the page, and I'm not all that sure I will be able to get him on the page in the first place anyway, and then if I do somehow by hook or by crook manage to get even one little bit of him, even one little aspect of him down on the page, I'm not all that sure I can keep even that little bit of him there for long enough to do any of us any good at all, even if I do figure out something to do with him once I get him there, because, you see, everything would have to be just right, just exactly perfectly right, and it would have to stay that way, because the instant that everything wasn't just exactly perfectly right, then he would be gone just like that. Instantaneously. Absolutely. Irrevocably. Gone. Just like that. Because my father would not, he absolutely would not under any circumstances just sit around passively for the purposes of politeness or anything else and just tolerate things being less than perfectly just right. No, he would get right out of there and fast, and lots of times before he got right out of there he would just break things—just whatever things happened to be around—to show exactly how he felt about it—he would crash things to the ground so there would be absolutely no doubt as to where he stood on the matter, whatever the matter might be, because where and how he stood was an important issue for my father—or he would hack things into pieces or just destroy things utterly in one way or another and then fling them, just hurl them away from himself and out into the abyss of intolerable imperfections out there orbiting aimlessly, forever banished from his awareness and from his sight. And if he couldn't hurl the things away from himself, then he would hurl himself away from the things that weren't just right and out of the scene at hand right that instant, right that very moment, as though he might almost will himself magically into another universe. Like, for example, it might be that a friend of his whom he had known for thirty years and whom he might have thought was a lot like himself, since they had gone to high school together, or it might be that they had both spent the war in hospitals or something like that, and it might be that my father and this friend of his would be sitting in a country-club dining room with starched white tablecloths or even in a café on the border with Mexican waiters in aprons standing around, and this friend might just inadvertently say something that might strike my father as indicating a fundamental breach of some kind, or maybe he would think it indicated some sort of betrayal or personal insult, as he was constantly on the alert for indications of these kinds, and then my father would just shoot from his chair, knocking it backward, would throw the wooden table with all its cutlery and crystal to the floor, and then my father would just run, would just go charging out of the room as fast as he possibly could in that stiff-legged walk he had, and then he might never speak to that old friend of his again, just to show that that was how strongly he felt about it. And suffering the consequences of showing how he felt about it was something that it seemed to me he didn't mind doing, and the fact that people didn't know what to do with him or how to handle the situations that he would cause didn't seem to bother him, as if that was something that was just in his body, as if the way he lived in his body was such that he had to show and act out everything. As if that was just a fact of reality and what other people chose to do about it was their own affair. Even when he was sitting in a chair, his fingers would be running and tapping and drumming to the rhythm of something inside him.

I remember looking at his left hand one day, the way you would look at the hand of a stranger on the subway—secretly spying on the hand while the stranger was looking in another direction—stealthily I was observing that small innocent creature—my father's left hand with its short fingers, the small clean nails, the pink skin with the brown freckles across the back. He had small hands for a man of his size—people used to say that when he was young and would get into fights his small hands were a problem for him. His hands looked to me like a boy's hands. They seemed to belong to someone I didn't know, not the person that we would all be so afraid of when he came home from work on a bad day and came charging into the house from the garage and we would all be sitting or standing around in the kitchen or the den and we would have known from the way we'd heard his car hit the driveway and by the speed with which he would have made it to the back door in that not-exactly-limping-but-making-lurching-forward-look-purposeful walk we all three grew up imitating—we would know, we would just know the way you know when you swing a bat that this one's going to be a foul, and even though the bat hasn't even hit the ball yet, you know that it's too late already to change it and that there is nothing you can do, because it's all already in motion and this one is just going to be a foul. And that's mostly the way it would be with him—all you could do would be to just try to get out of the way in time, because when things weren't just right, sometimes he would fall down, because he had those bad feet, but usually he would just break things, like he would break ashtrays and dishes and glasses and chairs and windows and doors and locks on doors and just anything—he even broke his own bones a lot. Sometimes if my mother fixed dinner and everything wasn't just right, he would throw the corncobs on the floor, because there was no plate set out for them the way he wanted, or he would hurl a whole tomato aspic across the room, because he had to have something to chew on. But mostly my father liked to eat better than he liked most things. He would lunge into each bite of food as he ate, surrounding and attacking each forkful as though the act of taking a bite were an act of capture, and as he ate he would go faster and faster, as though accelerating toward some climactic moment, and sometimes as he did so, his eyes would seem to glaze, as though he were not only consuming but also being consumed, merging with something larger in which to be lost the way he told me one time he was lost in the morphine they gave him when his feet were crushed in the first place and he spent years in hospitals like the one at Valley Forge, where I saw him for the first time I can remember seeing him and knowing that he was my father, and he was all bound up in a cast that covered his whole body, and I heard he later cut that cast off himself and went running around like he wasn't supposed to do, and he hurt himself, and they didn't know what to do with him and they had to put him in a new cast. He was always hurting himself, but he didn't seem to care about that, because he wanted to have things a certain way. Like when they operated on his feet the first time and he wouldn't have a general anesthetic, because they wouldn't promise him that they wouldn't cut off the worse of the feet, because they said he would never walk on them because of the pain, but he wouldn't let them do it, and so after that he made himself walk, but the feet were always hurting—especially that one worse foot—and he was constantly moving them, like if we would go to a movie, he wouldn't just sit there but he would be up and down and up and down the whole time, getting popcorn and drinks and going to the bathroom and just walking around, and while he was sitting there in his seat, his feet would be moving up and down in the aisle, or his knees would be going back and forth and back and forth, and lots of times something in the movie wouldn't be just right, so we would all have to get up and leave right in the middle. Even when he was sitting at home and watching TV, it would be the same way. He would be moving his feet up and down the whole time, pumping them up and down and back and forth in those dark brown, lace-up, oxford-type shoes. The shoes would always have to be of the softest leather, and always the best and sometimes handmade, and they must have been a lot of trouble to find, because one of his feet was a different size and shape than the other foot since the war, so he usually had to either buy two pairs—one for one foot and one for the other—or he had to have them specially made to measure, but then his feet hurt all the time anyway. He would keep on moving those feet up and down and back and forth, and they were so stiff and so square that they looked almost like wooden feet, and he walked on them and used them in a way that seemed to me to be just as if they were wooden feet, because the ankles didn't move, so they had this stiff look, and if you could see them without shoes and without those thin dress socks he would always wear, then you would see how stiff and wasted and white and woodish they appeared, and why he walked on them as if he were walking on stilts—except that in a way they were stilts that had been fashioned in the early days of plastic surgery and were made of bone and flesh and also nerves, with those pink raised scars all around the tendons and the square heels and the ankles, which were bony and lumpy in an undefined sort of way—like man-made approximations of feet. And his feet were always getting injured and reinjured, like the time when my parents went to Nassau with their friends and my father didn't believe them when they said there were stinging sea urchins on the beach, and so he wound up with a swollen foot full of stinging sea-urchin quills, as well as with a bad sunburn, because he also didn't believe that he couldn't stay out in the sun as long as anyone with his redhead's skin, and so the next day he was stuck in his hotel room while everyone else was out on the beach again, and he didn't know what to do with himself all day, and he got curious about the little metal trapdoor that was in the ceiling of the bathroom of his hotel room, so he found a screwdriver and undid all four screws and the metal trapdoor fell corner-down right on the instep of his now triply injured foot, so he wound up in another hospital.

I remember when they came back from that trip and he was so angry and breaking things every day, and he paced up and down the kitchen on one cane and ate three whole packages of Nestle's cooking chocolate, and when he did that, he got this look on his face that I remembered seeing when I was a very small child and I saw him pull a bottle out of the wood-bin that was in the brick fireplace, and he turned that bottle up, and as he drank, he lunged toward that bottle with his face—he lunged into it as though he were Alice plunging in that instant through some looking-glass boundary in his own mind, and his face seemed to me to have the look of standing in a strong wind. And it was way back then when I was small that things were the worst with the drinking and with the feet, like during the time when he was in the leg casts and he couldn't get around except on heavy wooden crutches, so there wasn't much he could do except make models of boats and planes and tanks and things, and there was this one model boat he was working on for a long time, and he would sit for hours absorbed in working on it and not moving very much at all, and it was a good one made of balsa wood, and then one day there was a piece he couldn't find and the boat was almost finished and he couldn't get that piece and he couldn't get it and he couldn't get anyone else to get it right that minute, and he got so mad that he just took his crutch and smashed that model boat into bits and pieces, and then it was ruined, and he had really liked that boat too and had been working on it for a long time and had bought the dope to paint it with and it was going to be blue and gray and red, and I had helped him to pick out the colors, but then he had crunched it into lots of pieces and it couldn't be put back together, and he had ruined everything. I didn't want to talk to him much for a long time after that, which made him even madder.

After the casts came off, he went from the crutches to using two canes, and his feet hurt a lot then and he had a hard time learning to balance on those two canes and would fall down a lot, such as the time when he had the two canes and it was dark and it was raining and the car lights and the streetlights were shiny on the pavement like streaky-colored mirrors, and we were all hurrying, and my mother said to him, Don't cross now, you'll fall. And the look he gave her, I thought he was going to hit her, but instead he leaned on those two thin canes with all his weight and he lunged into the street, and it was raining hard and there were cars, and he went thumping across as fast as he could, and he went lurching across as well as he could, but his weight was on those two thin cane tips, and one slid out from under him and he fell down hard, slipping and sliding in the street, and cars screeched and skidded on the mirrored wet pavement, and he glared right into their grills, baring his teeth and yelling and cursing, and then he looked back at my mother and me as if we were the same as the car grills, and then he struggled up, saying not to help him, goddammit, and to get away from him, and then he hit at the car nearest with one of the canes, and then he took off his nice new overcoat, which was now all wet and grease-stained, and he threw it in the street, and then he was mad and wouldn't talk to anyone for the rest of the night. I was getting to where I didn't want to talk to him all that much either, and not too long after that, when it was my fifth or sixth birthday, he gave me a pair of tall wooden stilts, and he made a point of saying that I had to learn to use them all by myself, but I never did, and I can still see those red-and-green-painted stilts leaning reproachfully against the back wall of the garage—and then months and even years later he would once in a while get this look in his eye, and he would ask me why I never learned to use those stilts.

After that, he went back to the surgeons and said that he had changed his mind and that he wanted them to go ahead and amputate that one of those feet that was always hurting him the most, but at that point he could already walk, so they refused to do it, and so he had to live with himself like that. Sometimes that one worse foot would bother him so much that he would go back to using one crutch around the house, just for a week or two. During one of the times while he was doing this and I was about five or six and I didn't want to go to school and was hiding out in the back yard hoping they would just forget about me for long enough that I could skip school for just that one day, and my mother was yelling around the house for me and was getting mad, and finally she started yelling out the back door for me, and then my father came clumping out, still in his bathrobe and on that one crutch, and he was furious that I would dare to defy them like that. I realized that I had made a big mistake, and I hunched down behind the newly cut woodpile, hoping that he wouldn't see me, but after calling out a couple of times, he headed straight for me, and I could see him through the spaces between the stacked logs near the top of the pile, and I was looking around for an escape, and then his crutch sank into the ground and he fell. He fell heavily, right into some uncut branches, and scraped his hand and arm. If I lifted up just a little, I could see him through the woodpile furiously struggling with his legs and feet and with his bathrobe and the crutch, and his face turning redder and redder, and then he picked up a hatchet that had been left by the uncut wood and he started hitting at his crutch with it. He got up on his one knee and hacked and hacked at that crutch, and he was chopping it in two. And I hunched down low behind the woodpile, and he just kept on hacking and hacking and hacking, and it seemed as if he had forgotten about me and about the yard and even about the crutch and everything, and that all he was thinking about was the hacking that went on and on, and then there was another sound—a worrying, whining sound that was deep and desperate, like the sound of an animal trying to get out of a trap, and it went on and on, and there was no other place for me to hide, and then everything stopped. Suddenly all the sounds stopped. I got up slowly to where I could peer between the logs and see him, and I could see that he had stopped hacking and was looking at the foot that was right there in front of him—it was the worse one of the two, and he was just staring at that foot with that hatchet in his hand, and that was when I knew that I had to get out of there right that minute, and so I jumped up and ran out from behind the woodpile and across the yard, and that was when my father looked up and saw me.

Old Enough

I can tell you what it's like to be left for a younger woman. For a long time, I couldn't. I could have told you what it was like to be left for another woman, but not for a younger one.

I was once, in fact, the younger woman a man left his wife for. Now you can argue (as I did at the time) that no one actually leaves one person for another. Something is already amiss between the original couple or no one would be looking for a reason, a person, to leave. You can make a case of that, but it's a crock. The fact is, he was living with his wife in some sort of peace, they had three children too young to go to school, he met me, he fell in love with me, he left his wife and three children to take up with me, and I thought the whole thing was incredibly romantic. It was the beginning of summer and I thought our love was destiny. I felt pretty smug about it all (although, of course, it was a shame about the kids), until a few months later when he told me, "It's not enough anymore." That was the end of summer, and I had learned a thing or two about destiny.

I remember the scene perfectly. He had come to my apartment, just a niche in a warren of niches carved in a solid old brick house that had once been home to a single family. Pecan trees darkened the narrow backyard and shaded the screened-in sleeping porch on the second floor; oleanders and altheas, unpruned and rangy, lifted their blossoms almost as high. Colored beads curtained the windows, an Indian spread covered my bed. Incense worthy of a papal High Mass wafted around me as I sat on the floor, listening for answers blowing in the wind.

He stood in front of me in this student-of-the-sixties Austin apartment and said, "It's not enough anymore." He began to explain at great length exactly what he meant, but I didn't hear a word of it. I was looking into his face thinking, "I'll be anything you want, I'll do anything you say. But once in a while let me know the warmth of your mouth, and once in a while let me feel the weight of your body on mine." Those were my exact thoughts—really—and I knew as I thought them that never since history began had such achingly beautiful sentiments filled a woman's heart. But at the time I wasn't even old enough to vote or buy beer, so I've learned to forgive myself.

So wrapped up was I in the purity of my sentiments that I did not immediately notice when he quit talking. I looked up to see his soft brown eyes upon me, expecting a reply, and I thought, "All that I am I have given to you. How can you say it's not enough?" I didn't say that, though. What I said was "Do you think that was fair? Was it fair of you to come to me with your ten years more and your broken marriage behind you and tell me there's such a thing as love?" He didn't answer. He only said once again, as though to repeat it were to make me understand, "I'm sorry, but it's not enough anymore." Then he turned and walked out the door.

Devastated, uncomprehending, I listened to his footsteps going through the kitchen, across the screened-in sleeping porch, and down the back steps. I listened as everything I cared about, everything that made life bearable, began walking down those steps, and I knew I had to stop him. I could not let him go. I was willing to plead, I was willing to beg, I was willing to kneel at his feet, but I had to do it before he turned the corner and walked out of my life forever.

My footsteps followed his through the kitchen, across the screened-in sleeping porch, and stopped at the top of the back steps. I saw him walking away from me—the black curly hair that had lain on my breast, his darling neck where my breath had lingered. I had wrapped my body and my life around him, and I stood at the top of the steps and prayed for words that would bring him back, words that would stop his flight, words that would carry him to my embrace.

If only I could find the right words, he would stop and turn. Our eyes would meet and I would run to him and he would enfold me in his arms. "Oh, my love," he would say as his lips brushed my hair. "What a fool I almost was." I would cry in my happiness and he would cry in his happiness and we would cry in each other's happiness. I would wrap my body and my life around him and there would never again be discord between us. But I had to have just the right words.

Inspiration hardly less than divine seized me. "Shane!" I called after him. "Shane! Come back!" He didn't stop. He didn't even turn around. He never could take a joke. But I thought it was hysterical. I sat down on the top step and laughed until I cried.

I figured it was all my fault. I had been too intense. (I was clearly off the track there. He had not, after all, said, "It's too much." I would tell you what he did say, but it has slipped my mind for the moment.) Yes, I had been intense, but only because I had found true love, which at the time I thought was the same as everlasting love. I loved him so much I had written him a poem which I left on my pillow one morning when I went to class before he woke up. Here is the poem, in its entirety:

> Man beside me that I love—
> Sleeping now—
> When you wake up,
> Will you remember
> Me?

Believe it or not, I spent quite a bit of time on that poem. Not so much on writing it, but on whether or not to capitalize the first letter of every line, whether or not to start all the lines flush left, whether or not to make the first line all one word. Twenty years later I am well aware that this poem might have initiated the beginning of the end. The man had his faults, but he was a professor of English.

Or it could have been the retainer imitation. I had begun to speak with my tongue adhered to the top of my mouth in imitation of a friend who had gotten a retainer. It drove my beloved crazy. He asked me repeatedly to stop, and I really tried to, but I had spent so much time perfecting the technique that I spoke that way without realizing it. He got tired of being addressed as "Schweechhearch." He had no appreciation for the skill involved. He thought it was stupid. He never actually said, that day when he left, "It's the retainer imitation," so I can't know for sure, but I had to entertain it as a possibility. It certainly made a lot more sense than the ridiculously ambiguous "It's not enough anymore," or any other feeble excuse I could think of, such as maybe he had quit liking me.

"Well," I thought, "I guess he's going off to be alone and be introspective, to find out about himself, where he's coming from, where he's going." I thought he was going off to get his head together, as we said back then. He probably needed to do that, I reasoned, after several years of marriage and a relationship which, although brief, had been one of the world's great romances.

One thing he had definitely not said was "There's someone else." Which is why I was so surprised, the very next day, to see him walking across campus with his arm around a girl who was neither myself nor his ex-wife, but someone whose peasant blouse fluttered with the rise and fall of her large, unfettered breasts and whose full and naturally blonde hair grazed her sun-bronzed thighs just below the ragged edge of her cutoffs. White trash if I'd ever seen it.

So being the woman another woman was left for was followed closely by being left for another woman, and if it wasn't the greatest time I've ever had I did learn a few things from the experience. I learned that saying, "Oh, my darling," during sex is not the same as looking into your loved one's soul. See, I thought it was, and the fact that it is not was such a revelation to me that I have never since said, "Oh, my darling," during sex. It's not that I don't talk. Sure I talk. I say, "Oh, my God, that's fantastic," or "No, no, no, you're doing it all wrong," but never again have I said, "Oh, my darling."

I also learned never to ask, "What are you thinking about?" This lesson was taught to me one sultry summer afternoon as we lay together in the tangled after-throes of passion. "What are you thinking about?" I asked as, with one finger, I traced the circles of his curls. "My wife," he answered. That was the last time I ever asked that question, and I'm always amazed when someone asks it of me. "How can you ask that?" I want to say. "Don't you know someone might tell you the truth someday?"

But the most important thing I learned was to be the one who leaves first. It's a lot easier to be the one walking out the door than it is to be the one standing at the top of the steps yelling, "Shane!" I tell you true. So I learned to be wary, to watch for the signs, to make an early exit. This can be a little self-defeating at times, breaking up with someone just when you start to like him, but you can't afford to let sentiment creep into your life and cloud your thinking.

Yes, I learned my lessons. I kept them in mind as the years passed. And the years did pass. Then one day it happened, just like in the movies. I fell in love again. It was one of the world's great romances. The word "forever" reentered my vocabulary. I became a believer. Friend, I was born again.

But destiny had a few more lessons to teach me, and ten years after I moved in (to the day, to the very day), I moved out. I gave him three months to come around. At the end of three months he had not come around. He was probably bluffing, but I couldn't live without him. I called him. I saw him. He told me he had started seeing someone else. I almost threw up.

A week later he called and asked to see me. He picked me up from work and we strolled along the Colorado River, joggers and bicyclists and dogs chasing Frisbees passing us on either side. I used to take friends there and point out the landmarks: "We were sitting on this bench when he told me he wanted to try again"; "Under that tree he said, 'After I saw you the other day, spending time with her just didn't make any sense.'" It's a lovely walk, especially if you go in early spring as he and I did. With the fruit trees flowering pink, rose, and red, and wisteria purpling the gazebos, I said yes, I'd love to try again.

I had him back. I had him back. My long, lean Texan. The sun made a crown of his curly gray hair and his eyes had never shone so blue in the burnished skin of his Cherokee ancestry. I kissed the backs of both his hands, his artist's hands that cooked all my meals, serenaded me on the ukulele, and carried me up to bed. I was very happy, not only because I was in love, but also because vindication carries its own rapture.

"Hah!" I thought. "She couldn't compete. She couldn't undo in three months what we spent years building. Hah!" I thought, and prepared to live happily ever after. But he didn't quit seeing her, which is why I call that path along the Colorado River where you can always find joggers and bicyclists and dogs chasing Frisbees "The Heartbreak Trail."

For some reason he had told me where she worked. I guess he thought it was important that I know. I called the people I knew who worked at the same place and said to them, "I don't want to know anything about her. I don't even want to hear the sound of her name." I had hardly hung up the phone before this girl had no secrets from me. My friends (my *friends,* can you imagine?) couldn't wait to tell me everything about her. I knew where she was born, where she was living. I knew where she went to church! I'm only surprised no one told me her sign.

"She's not as attractive as you," they said. ("Oh, thanks. I got thrown over for a dog.") "He gave her a ring for her birthday," they said. ("Is that so? He never gave me a ring for my birthday." Mind you, he gave me many lovely things, among them a heart on a chain which I took off the day I left and never put back on although I used to clutch it in my hand as I cried myself to sleep each night, and isn't that the most achingly beautiful thing you've ever heard? But the point here is that he gave her a ring and he never gave me one. If he had given her tropical fish I would have remembered he never gave me tropical fish and I would have felt injured about that.)

I handled it all pretty well until they told me her age. I won't tell you her exact age, but I'll give you a hint: it's a number that starts with a one. To say I went to pieces suggests I took it a lot more bravely than I did. To say I lost my composure sets something of a standard for understatement.

In fact, I cried for six months. I don't mean I cried off and on for six months. I mean I cried every day for the next six months. I woke up crying. I cried while I dressed for work. I cried while I drove to work. I cried at the copy machine. I sat in my car and cried during my lunch hour. I cried myself to sleep each night. I woke up in the middle of the night crying. And as I cried, I called his name.

Whenever I started to feel a little better, when, for instance, I had gone a couple of hours without crying, I would see them drive by in his car. Them. Him and her. You know who I mean. He had a convertible, the top of which he never put up, so there was no mistaking who they were. They were the happy couple in the convertible. There was no mistaking me, either. I was the solitary figure watching through eyes swollen to slits as they drove past, spitting their exhaust fumes in my face.

But don't think that, demented though I was by weeping, the irony of the situation escaped me. Don't think I didn't recognize that things had come full circle. Don't think I failed to realize that she was about the age I had been in my younger-woman days while I . . . well, I was old enough to be A Wife.

I remember the night I counted backwards on my fingers to figure out how old she had been when my former—her current—lover and I started living together. By my calculations, when my former—her current—lover and I started living together, going to the prom was one of her distant dreams.

I thought then of my counterpart, the wife I had supplanted. Had she too counted backwards on her fingers to see how old I had been when she got married? Could she picture me among the flower girls at her wedding, a basket of rose petals in my hands, a garland of ribbons in my hair, while she stood smiling at her handsome groom? Well, I finally knew how she felt, more or less, because of course I didn't have three towheaded children sitting at my feet while I counted backwards on my fingers, a distinction for which I was grateful. Still, I knew what it was like to watch the man you love walk off with jailbait.

When I first started crying I wasn't too worried. "Okay," I thought, "this is the really hard part and it lasts about a month. I'll cry endlessly for a month and then it will start to get better." So I cried endlessly for a month and it didn't get better. I cried for another month, and another, and another, and another. At the end of six months I felt just as bad as I had the day I found out about her.

"So," my friends said, "why don't you fight for him?" Now how do you fight for someone? What was I supposed to do—start wearing perfume? This man knew me. He knew whether or not he wanted me. And he had made it perfectly clear that he didn't. It's hard to fight for a man when he refuses to see you. My best friend had the best suggestion: "Hit her on the back of the head with a rock," she said.

My worst fear was that he would die loving her. I know that sounds pathetic—it *is* pathetic—but he certainly wasn't going to outlive her.

Thus I came to understand the difficulties people face in turning thirty or thirty-five or forty or whatever milestone birthday might be approaching. Thus I learned how unsettling such an event can be. My birthdays had had very little effect on me. I was perennially young. Everyone said so. "You haven't changed a bit," people who hadn't seen me in years would say. I was short, I was thin, I was elfin, so what was this business about aging, anyway?

Someday, perhaps, I would begin to look older. I might even begin to feel older. When that happened, I would accept it gracefully. My face, like those of the ancient and weathered Indian women whose photographic portraits are so admired, would be etched with the story of my life. It would be a strong face, a wise face, a face finally old, yet forever young. (Although I must admit I have yet to see anyone walk up to the Estée Lauder counter in a department store and say, "I'll buy whatever it takes to make me look like an eighty-five-year-old Navajo.")

If I had forgotten the power that comes with being nineteen, there were constant reminders. It's hard to get away from them if you live in Austin. One day, in a feast of masochism, I went to the University of Texas campus just to do a comparison. I wanted to make sure they were different from me. They were.

They were beautiful, those girls. Looking at them, I remembered the summer I was nineteen, when every man who met me fell in love with me. I remembered men turning to look at me, not because I was beautiful, which I have never been, but simply because I was nineteen. I remembered the power and the aura of that age, when you think a wonderful life lies ahead of you. You think everything will go just the way you want it to. You think that magical summer will last forever, and that all your life, men will turn to look at you. Watching those girls on campus, seeing them as competitors, I could have fallen in love with some of them myself.

Now I don't necessarily think that one day the man I loved looked at me and said, "She's too old." But when you get left for a teenager you have to conclude that if a man is interested in perfect muscle tone, there's not a lot you can do about it.

I tried to bring a bit of humor to the situation. I am, after all, known for my ability to bring humor to a situation. I told people I was going to make a tee shirt that said, "Old enough to be left for a younger woman." And I tried to stop crying. I tried very hard. I tried pulling myself up by my bootstraps, keeping a stiff upper lip, looking for the silver lining. I tried talking sternly to myself. "Oh, grow up," I said to myself sternly. "Would you rather have varicose veins?" And then I would start to cry again. I began to wonder if my eyes would ever not be bloodshot, if my face would ever not be swollen, if my nose would ever recover from facial-tissue burn.

Then one day I didn't cry. I cried the next day and for several days after that, but there had been that one day I hadn't cried. A couple of weeks later, I didn't cry again. Some days I was awake for five or ten minutes before I thought of him and her and how old I was, when of course I would start to cry again, but at least I didn't wake up crying, which is not an auspicious way to begin the day. Then there started to be more days when I didn't cry than days when I did, and now it's been a long time since I cried. Years.

I met her some time after all this happened, when it didn't matter anymore. (We worked together, she and I. Is this a story of the eighties, or what?) My friends had been right—she's not as attractive as I am. But what shocked me, what made me stare at her when she didn't know I was looking, was that there was about her nothing of youth. Where had she found that suit that a middle-aged banker would shun? And her graceless, lumbering walk—had that set his fingertips tingling?

She had, of course, gotten older. She was, at last, out of her teens. But she was still young. She was still a girl. So where were the aura and the power? I don't suppose I'll ever know, because it was hardly the kind of thing I could discuss with her. But it certainly left me wondering who was the May and who the December in their romance.

If I had seen her at the start, perhaps I would not have had to face the loss of my youth. I could have saved that crisis for my fortieth birthday. If I had seen her at the start, perhaps I would not have responded to an issue that didn't exist. But I mistook youth for the issue and I learned the wrong lesson. I learned that I was no longer young, when I could have learned that I'm a fool for love, or that my life was not to resemble Jane Eyre's. Or I might even have learned that it's not always best to be the one to leave.

I will tell you that, some time after I stopped crying, he came to see me. I was living in Travis Heights by then, growing my own cilantro and determining my moral stance on the Salvation Army's plan to move to South Austin. He sat next to me on the porch swing and watched while I snapped beans into a Tupperware bowl. Tapping a foot against the wooden floor I set the swing in motion, and as it carried us in and out of the shadows of the live oak trees, he told me how sorry he was and he asked me to come back.

Luckily I am a person of great emotional maturity and hence derived absolutely no satisfaction from this encounter. I simply stared into my bowl of beans and declined the offer in passionless language that did not include the words "nyah, nyah, nyah."

I don't mean to say it was easy for me. If I was no longer crying about the loss of love and of youth, I hadn't started laughing about it either. And I was glad he had not asked me sooner. I was glad he had not asked me sooner when I might have said yes and faced a lifetime of becoming ill whenever a woman 365 days younger than I approached.

I rose from the swing and watched as he walked down the steps—the curly gray hair that had lain on my breast, his darling neck where my breath had lingered, his artist's hands that would never again frame my face as he bent to kiss me—and I didn't yell "Shane!" and I didn't say "nyah, nyah, nyah." You do learn a few things with age.

I did have that tee shirt made. I wear it when I jog the Heartbreak Trail. People running toward me smile as they see "Old enough to be left for a younger woman." They can read on my back as I blaze past, "Young enough not to care."

ROBERT FLYNN

The Midnight Clear

She was almost thirty-seven and out of time. Like others she had wanted children, a husband, a home. Like others she had a hope chest, embroidered dreams, crocheted illusions. Like others she had expectations. She wanted a man who was clean, polite but not fawning, educated but not vain about it, gentle but not weak, not given to snuff or overly given to alcohol, sloth, and smiling at women. In two months she would be up to hopeless, and her expectations down to clean.

At her feet, under the still fresh mound of dirt and already dusty bits of ribbon was her father. A hard man—some said selfish. A religious man—some said self-righteous. Her mother had died when she was twelve and she had taken on her mother's work of taking care of him. He frequently quoted the Bible regarding a virtuous woman and a daughter's duty towards her father.

Standing over his grave, she felt an emptiness in the place where duty had been, a sadness where love had been, a pain where anger had been, and a blank where hope had been. She shook the dust off the ribbons and retied them to the wooden cross where she had placed them for a bit of color. She had taken the ribbons off the Christmas tree. Her father wasn't much for frivolity but being a Christian he let her decorate a Christmas tree. It was still five days until Christmas but she wouldn't be needing the ribbons. Or the tree. She had been loved and ill-used. Now she was alone.

He was almost forty-five and almost out of luck. Like others he had wanted a piece of land, a strong, healthy wife, and a passel of hearty, handy kids to help with the work. Like others he had prospects—a Peter Shutter wagon, a good team of mules, and the money. Like others he had expectations—a woman old enough not to be flighty, not too old to work and have kids; girl enough to be tenderhearted but woman enough not to be weepy; not so pretty as to be spoiled or so ugly as to be mean; not too fast out of bed to be a comfort, or too slow to have coffee ready by first light when it was time to go to work; not so big as to be clumsy or so small as to be worthless with mules or the bearer of children too small to handle posthole diggers.

At his feet, under the still-fresh mound of dirt and the flowers and feathers he had taken off her hats, was his wife. She had been pretty—some said frail. She had been cheerful—some said giddy. She had told him she loved him and sung him songs while the biscuits burned, the garden went undug, and he had to hire a hand to help him castrate his calves, survey his fence lines, and scald his hogs.

Standing over her grave he felt emptiness where the impatience had been, grief where the love had been, emptiness where the disappointment had been, dead where the dreams had been. He had been loved but not helped, and now he was alone.

*   *   *

He noticed her because she was crying softly and trying to retie the red and green ribbons so they did not tangle in the wind. She was healthy. She noticed him because he had tears in his eyes and was trying to keep the little bouquet of feathers and flowers from blowing off the grave. He was clean. She stood and the ribbons tangled until they looked like something that had been discarded. He stood up and the feathers blew away and the flowers rolled up at his feet.

"I got a hammer and some nails in the wagon if that will help you," he said, holding his hat in his hand. He had feelings.

"I'm obliged. I got a pin if you can use it," she said. She knew how to use a hammer.

She watched him as he gathered the feathers and flowers and deftly pinned them together. He had gentle hands.

He watched as she drove nails into the wooden cross and rearranged the ribbons. She was strong and definite.

"I got a little something to eat if you'd like a bite," she said. She had brought a basket from town. A generous woman.

"I got some water in the wagon," he said. "And two cups." A thoughtful man.

While they ate, they talked. He had sold everything he had and was on his way to Wanderer Springs. He had hung on longer than he had intended, waiting for his wife to get strong enough to move. "Time to make a new start," he said.

She had spent her life taking care of her father. "I ain't never been alone," she said.

"What was your wife like?" she asked.

"She was a good woman, but made for gentler use than I could afford. What was your pa like?"

"He meant to get the most out of what was his whether it was a horse or a mule, but he was fair. He expected the same from everybody."

"I got money for a good farm," he said. "I'm a hard

worker and a good farmer. I aim to get me a new wife and a passel of kids."

"I'm partial to kids," she said. "I ain't never been sick to speak of. I got all my teeth. I kept my own hens, weeded my own garden, milked my own cow, and helped Pa with the hitching, fencing, and loading."

"Would you be agreeable to marrying me?" he asked. His hat was in his hand again.

"I ain't never been married," she said.

"I ain't no fool boy to be rushing you," he said.

"How soon do you intend to start with the mothering and fathering?"

"I'd be willing to wait until we got to Wanderer Springs. It ain't but six days. If we got married today we could be there by Christmas." He turned and looked at the wagon, hitched and loaded and ready to go.

"Yes," she said. "I know where the preacher is. But it ain't but five days until Christmas."

They went by her house and got her hope chest, stood before the preacher, and started for Wanderer Springs with her holding a bouquet made of the funeral flowers and the Christmas ribbons, and her cow tied to the back of the wagon.

The first day they talked about the house. "Lean-to is easiest," he said.

"Not for kids," she said.

They settled on a lean-to until the well was dug, three rooms before the second child, a storm cellar when the barn was finished, a well house when the fences were done, and a porch before the second barn.

He stopped the wagon at dusk. He built a fire while she milked the cow. While she cooked, he unharnessed the team and staked them out with the cow. They ate quickly in silence using syrup bucket lids for plates. The hope chest would not be unpacked until there was a lean-to. She asked if he had enough to eat and he said yes.

While she scoured the dishes with clean sand, he brought up more firewood and got the blankets out of the wagon. He spread her blankets before the fire and took his to the other side of the wagon. She lay down, fully clothed, and rolled her back to the fire. She saw him watching her from his bed on the other side of the wagon.

"I'd like to be hitched by first light," he said.

"Will the smell of coffee wake you?" she asked.

The second day they talked about the children. The first boy would be named for her dead father. The first girl would be named for his dead wife. If there wasn't a school by the time the first child was ten they would mail-order books and instead of picking berries she would teach them to read, write, and add, cook, can, and milk. Instead of fishing, he would teach them time, calendar, planting and harvesting season, sawing, fencing, and water witching. That night they slept on opposite sides of the wagon but he asked if she had enough wood. She said yes.

The third day they talked church. "I'm Baptist," she said. "I don't tolerate dipping, drinking, or dancing."

"I'm agreeable to church but I ain't no particular brand," he said. "I don't chew or drink, I don't cuss unless I have to, and I ain't never had no time for dancing."

She wanted grace before meals and reading the Bible to the children before bed. She could say grace before meals, he would read the Bible to the children, but he would not sing, pray, or testify in front of a bunch of Baptists. She would tithe eggs and butter to the preacher, he would pledge corn or cash to the church. That night they slept on separate sides of the wagon but he asked if she was warm enough. She said yes.

"We'll be on our own land by Christmas," he said. "Three more days."

"Christmas is day after tomorrow," she said.

"Today is Wednesday," he said.

"Today is Thursday."

The next day they were discussing whether to cure ham or smoke it. He said he didn't like ham as dry as that coyote they saw yesterday.

"What coyote?"

"That dead coyote that we passed by that little draw."

"Surely you mean wolf," she said. "It wasn't full growned but it was a wolf."

"The one that was right there by the off-mule?" he said. "That was a coyote. I've knowed coyotes all my life."

"I was closer," she said.

For a while they sat in silence, listening to the grinding of the wheels, the jingle of the trace chains, the steady plodding of the mules. Then without a word he turned the wagon and they started on the back track. That night they slept on separate sides of the wagon.

The next day he clucked up the mules and they started up the back track. They didn't talk, lost in their own thoughts. He didn't want to be married to no stubborn, grudge-bearing woman. She didn't want to be married to no hard-headed man without the common sense to admit when he was wrong.

It was late afternoon when they reached the carcass and scavengers had scattered the bones. Both of them stood looking at it for a while and then he got the shotgun out of the wagon and started off down the draw. She got the axe and went in the opposite direction.

"I couldn't get no goose," he said. "All I got was a rabbit. I reckon that dog was chasing a rabbit when it died right over there."

"I'm partial to rabbit," she said. She propped up a salt cedar with rocks. She had decorated the tree with the ribbons and flowers from her bridal bouquet. "I got the tree ready 'cause we won't know when midnight comes," she said.

They ate the rabbit, and when they were finished, he said,

"I didn't have no time for a proper gift. I'd like our first girl to be named for you."

"I think that's the nicest present I ever got," she said. "We'll name the second one for your first wife."

She scoured the pots with sand and he built up the fire and got the bedding out of the wagon.

"I didn't have no time for a proper gift for you," she said, "but I'd be proud if you spread your bed by the fire."

He looked at her for a moment, then spread the beds side by side before the fire. "Don't worry none about coffee in the morning," he said.

WILLIAM GOYEN

Precious Door

For Reginald Gibbons

"Somebody's laying out in the field," my little brother came to tell us. It was eight o'clock in the morning and already so hot that the weeds were steaming and the locusts calling. For a few days there had been word of a hurricane coming. Since yesterday we had felt signs of it—a stillness of air followed by an abrupt billowing of wind; and the sky seemed higher, and it was washed-looking.

"Must be a drunken mill man sleeping in the weeds, or a hobo. Could even be your Uncle Bud, God knows," my father told me; "go see what it is."

"Come with me," I asked my father. "I'm scared."

What we found was a poor beaten creature who did not answer my father's calls. My father and I carried the unconscious person onto the back porch and laid him on the daybed.

"I wish you wouldn't let the children see that," my

mother said, and drew back into the darkness of the house like her own shell.

"He may be dying," my father said, "can't rouse him. Call the doctor, son, then get me some warm water. Hey," my father called loudly at first and then lowered his voice to a soft summons, "Hey, friend, hello; hello . . ."

The battered friend did not budge, but he was breathing, now quite heavily, almost gasping. The warm water cleaned away some of the blood that was like paste on his lips and cheeks, and then some cool water stroked back his dark hair from his brow; and we saw in that moment when his face and his look came clear to us what would have been called a beautiful young girl if it had been a girl; but it was a man. Something shining came through the damaged face and we knew we had brought a special person into our house out of the weeds of the field. When my father pulled back the stained shirt of the stranger and saw something, he told the children (I was twelve and the oldest) to go outside in the yard. I did not go far but hid under the yellow jasmine against the screen and listened.

"Pardner, you might not make it," I heard my father say, "if the doctor don't hurry up and get here. Because somebody's cut you with a knife." And in another moment I heard my father say, "Who did this to you? Cut you like this?" There was no sound from the wounded stranger. "Hanh?" my father murmured tenderly, "who hurt you like this? Hanh? He can't hear me or he can't talk. Well, you try to rest until the doctor comes," I heard my father say softly. At that moment I felt so sorry for this stranger lying silent in our house that I suddenly cried, there under the yellow jasmine.

The hurricane that was said to be coming toward us from down off the deep southern Gulf kept reaching at us. Now we could smell it; and quick wind, then rain, had turned over us, whipped away, turned back on us. Now it really was close on us and my father guessed we were going to get it. Storms scared my father where little else did. He felt afraid in our old house and always took us to the high school basement. "Mary, you and the children go on to the high school and hurry up," my father called. At this I rushed into the house.

"I'll stay with my father and the hurt man," I announced. There was going to be a discussion of this, but little time was left for it; and I could see that my father was glad to have me stay.

The storm came nearer. It threw down a limb of a hickory tree across the road and a driving rain hit against the side of our house for a few minutes, then stopped.

"It's coming," my father said. "We can't stay out here on this screen porch. Latch the screen door and move things away from the open. We'll move the hurt man into the parlor. What's your name, friend?" I saw my father put his ear to the young man's mouth.

My father lifted up the stranger and carried him like a child inside the house to the parlor, where few people went. It was a cool shadowy room used only for special occasions. It looked like my father wanted to give the wounded man the best we had to give.

I covered things on the porch and pushed things back and brought some firewood to the parlor. "I thought we could build a fire in the fireplace," I announced. "That'd be fine," my father said. "You know how to do it, like I taught you." I saw that he had made a pallet on the floor with the mattress from the daybed.

"Help me put our friend on the pallet," father asked.

When we lifted our friend I was at first afraid to touch him so close, to hold him, but in my trembling grasp his body felt friendly and like something of mine—and more: he felt beloved to me. He must have felt something of the same to my father, for I saw my father's face filled with softness in the light of the fire. Now the fire was going and brightness and warmth were coming from it, suddenly bringing to life on the wall the faces of my grandmother and grandfather who had built fires in this

71

fireplace; they looked down from their dusty frames upon us. Suddenly the man murmured, "Thank you."

"God bless you, pardner," my father said, and I patted the man's head. My breath was caught in my throat, that he was with us.

The storm was here, upon us. Our little house began to shudder and creak under it. Though we didn't say anything, my father and I were afraid that Doctor Browder would never be able to get out to us now; for when we could see what would be the dirt road in front of our house we saw a flowing stream; and when we saw in the lightning some trees fall over the road along the field we knew the doctor could not get to us.

We began to nurse the wounded stranger, my father and I. We washed his wounds. And my father prayed, there in the yellow firelight in the swaying little house my grandfather had built for his family and whose roof and walls and floor had been their safe haven and now ours, a shelter for generations in a world none of us had known beyond this place and a few nearby little towns. My father prayed over the young man, laying his carpenter's hand on the brow of the suffering man and clasping his hand in love and hope. And then I heard my father's words, "He's dead."

We said the Lord's prayer together on our knees by the dead stranger's pallet. The rhythmic clanging of the wind against something of metal, our washtub maybe, tolled over our prayer. And when we opened our eyes at the end of the prayer, my father said, "He looks like somebody." I knew he did, in that moment, for I saw in my sorrow his somehow blessed brow and his pale full lips, his dark bitter hair, familiar as kin. The wind tolled the washtub. My heart was heavy and aching and my face felt flooded but no tears came for a long time. And when they came, I sobbed aloud. My father held me and rocked me as though I were three, the way he used to when I was three; and I heard him cry, too.

I felt for the first time the love that one person might have for another he did not know, for a stranger come suddenly close. The great new swelling love I had for the stranger visitor to our house now filled our parlor. And I hoped then, with a longing that first touched me there on that wild and tender night in our faraway parlor in that hidden little town, that one day I would know the love of another, no matter how bitter the loss of them would be.

In the toiling hurricane that whipped at our house, our trees and fields, lightning showed us what the storm had already done to the world outside. "This must be the worst ever to hit this country," my father said. "God hold down our roof over our heads and receive the spirit of this poor man."

"And protect Mama and Sister and Joe in the school basement," I added.

The flood rose to our front porch. My father and I sat lone with the stranger. My father had washed him and taken away his clothes that had been stained again by his wounds and dressed him in a fresh shirt and workpants. The dead being was a presence in the parlor. We waited.

The sun flared out and streamed down on the waters that covered the town in the unsettled midafternoon. We looked out and saw a whole world of things floating by. We ourselves felt afloat, among them. And then the rain began again, right out of the sunshine, and put it out. It turned very dark.

"We're lost," my father told me. "We'll all be washed away."

"God please stop the rain," I prayed. The fire had burnt our supply of wood and it was sinking fast.

"Go get a candle from the bedroom, son," my father asked. "We'll put it by the body so that it won't lie in the darkness."

When my father called the stranger "the body" I felt, for the first time, a sense of death and loss. Our friend whom I loved and grieved for, as though I had long known him, was gone. Only "the body" remained. Now I understood the hardest part of death, the grief at gravesides, and what was given up there so bitterly. It was the body.

What interrupted our mourning was a figure at the window. A figure of flying hair and tearing clothes with wild eyes and a face of terror stared through veils of water.

"Somebody," I gasped to my father. "Somebody wants in from the storm."

"Hot damn Lord help us!" my father cried out, as afraid as I had ever seen him.

We struggled with the front door. When we unlocked it, it blasted against us and knocked us down to the floor, and it seemed to hurl the blowing figure into the house. We saw that it was a young man in tattered clothes and a thick beard. The three of us were able to close the front door and to barricade it with the heavy hat tree, oaken and immemorial, standing in the same place in the hallway since first my eyes found it. Suddenly it had life.

"Worst storm I've ever seen," my father said to the man. The man nodded and we could see that he was young.

When he walked into the parlor, drawn there by the candlelight and the fire, he saw the man on the pallet and lunged to it and fell to his knees and cried out and wept over the dead man. My father and I waited with our heads bowed, holding together in bewilderment under the fire's guttering sound and the soft sobbing of the young man. Finally my father said, "He was lying in the field. We tried to help him." But the man stayed on his knees beside the figure on the pallet, sobbing and murmuring. "Boy, boy, boy, boy . . ."

Then my father went to the kneeling man and put a blanket around his shoulders and said softly,

"I'll get some hot coffee, pardner."

I was alone with the two men, dead and alive, and I felt scared but full of pity. I heard the man speak softly, now, in a gasping language I could not understand—or I was too choked with astonishment. And then I heard him say clearly, "Put your head on my breast, boy! Here. Now, now boy, now; you're all right, now. Head's on my breast; now, now."

When my father came into the parlor with coffee, he put it down at the side of the grieving man. "Sit back, now," he said, "and warm yourself."

When the man sat back and pulled the blanket around his shoulders, my father asked him for his name.

"Ben," he said. "He and I are brothers. I brought him up." He would not drink his coffee but looked down at the figure of his brother and said, "We were in the boxcar comin from Memphis. Goin to Port of Houston. We had a plan." And then he cried out softly, "I didn't go to hurt him. I swear to God I didn't mean to hurt him." And then he held his brother's head to his breast and rocked him.

My father and I were sitting on the cold springs of the daybed whose mattress was the dead man's pallet, and I could feel the big, strong wrap of my father's arm around me, pulling my head to his breast. I felt my everlasting love for him, my father, but in my head rang Ben's words, *we had a plan*. My blood rushed in exciting hope. And that hope was that one day I would have enough courage to be this tender as this man was now at this moment, if ever I was lucky enough to find someone who would take my tenderness. And to have, together with someone, a plan. I knew, at this moment, that that was the thing I would look for in my life. And who could hold that from me or tell me I could not have it, that unspeakable tenderness that already I felt to grow in my breast as my blood rushed through me and which was the gift of Ben and his brother to me.

And out of this passion, as though I had been blinded by it and now could see again, I saw Ben lifting up the body of his dead brother from the pallet.

"Thank you for tending to my brother," he said to us,

solemnly, and turned to go. "My brother and me will go, now."

"But you'll drown," my father told him. "Wait until the flood is over, for God's sake."

My father stood in front of Ben as if to stop him; but in a growling voice and with a look of darkness, Ben said,

"Get out of our way, my friend."

Ben was going, holding the nestled body against his breast. My father and I stood still as our visitors out of the flood went back into it, through the barricaded front door and into the storm.

"Goodbye, goodbye," I whispered.

"God be with you and God forgive me for letting a man who killed his brother go," my father said, almost to himself.

Through the window we saw, in the fading daylight, the brothers move through the water. Ben was nestling the body of his dead brother in his arms and pressing his head upon his breast. "They'll never make it," my father said.

"But where are they going?"

"They're in God's hands," answered my father. "Although Ben was a murderer, I feel he is forgiven because he came back and asked forgiveness," father said. "The love of God works through reconciliation."

"Father," I asked. "What is reconciliation?"

"It means coming back together in peace," my father answered. "Although there was torment between the two brothers, they have been brought back together in peace."

Through the gray rain, moving through the rising waters, they disappeared, the two men of "reconciliation" who had come back together in peace. My eyes clung to them as long as they could see, trying to hold the loving enemy brothers back from the mist they were slowly melting into.

The days after the rain were worse than the rain. The river swelled and covered farms and roads and many people sat on top of their houses. Though the water around us fell to the lower land, since we were on a rise, my father and I were marooned. The sun had a new hotness, the world was sodden and the smell was of soaked things and rotting things. There were snakes and sobbing bullfrogs and there were crying peafowls in the trees and red crawfish flipped in the mud. In the remoteness and seclusion of our place, through the strangeness of our days, I wept for Ben and his brother so many times I can't remember. A new feeling had been born in me, obscure then but clearer through time. A man in a boat stopped to tell us of the wonders of the storm: gin cotton lay over an acre of water like white flowers; a thousand sawmill logs were aloose, a church steeple had been carried away with its bell, miraculously afloat, and stood gonging like a buoy near Trinity bridge.

And for a while it was reported that a floating door bearing the bodies of two men was seen moving on the wide river through several towns. At one town people had said that when it came through there, the raft was whirling in the currents as though a demon had hold of it; but the men stayed put, though it was considered that they were dead. And another time, near the river's mouth where it flows into the Gulf, they said it rode the crests of dangerous rapids so serenely that it was easy to see the two men, one, alive and fierce, holding the other, dead. I waited to hear more, but after this, there were no further reports of the precious door.

The Texas Principessa

Who would've dreamed that I would get the Palazzo? Well let me try and stay on what you asked me about before we were so rudely interrupted—by me. That ever happen to you? Start out to tell one thing and get off onto another? Well let me try and stay on what you asked me about. Welcome to the Palazzo.

The Texas Principessa had married a Naples Prince of an old line. Hortense Solomon (we called her Horty) was herself of an old line—of dry goods families. Texas Jews that had intermarried and built up large stores in Texas cities over the generations. Solomon's Everybody's Store was an everyday word in the mouths of Texas people and an emporium—which was their word—where Texas people were provided with everything from hosiery to clocks. The Solomons, along with the Linkowitzes, the Dinzlers and the Myrons, were old pioneers of Texas. They were kept to their faith by traveling Rabbis in early days, and later they built Synagogues and contributed Rabbis and Cantors from their generations—except those who married Texas Mexicans or Texas Frenchmen. These, after a while, melted into the general mixture of the Texas population and ate cornbread instead of bagels and preferred barbeque pork and tamales to lox and herring. That ever happen to you? Let's see where was I?

Oh. The Naples Prince, Renzi da Filippo, did not bring much money to the marriage because the old line of da Filippos had used up most of it or lost it; or had it taken from them in one way or another—which was O.K. because they had taken it from somebody else earlier on: sometimes there is a little justice. That ever happen to you? Renzi was the end of the line. Someone who was the end of a line would look it, wouldn't you think so? You could not tell it in Renzi da Filippo, he looked spunky enough to *start* something; he was real fresh and handsome in that burnt blond coloring that they have, sort of toasted—toast-colored hair and bluewater eyes and skin of a wheaty color. He was a beauty everyone said and was sought after in Rome and London and New York. Those Italianos! About all he had in worldly goods was the beautiful Palazzo da Filippo in Venice, a seventeenth-century hunk of marble and gold that finally came into his hands. Had Hortense Solomon not given her vows to Renzi in wedlock, Palazzo da Filippo might have gone down the drain. It needed repair in the worst kind of way—all those centuries on it—and those repairs needed a small fortune—which Horty had a lot of. As soon as the marriage was decided upon, there was a big party. The Prince was brought to Texas and an announcement party was thrown, and I mean *thrown,* on the cold ranch river that flowed through the acres and acres of hot cattleland owned by the Solomons. The gala stirred up socialites as far as Porto Ercole and Cannes, from which many of the rich, famous and titled flew in on family planes. Horty Solomon—which was very

80

hard for Italians to say so they called her La Principessa di Texas—started right in with her plans for fixing up the Palazzo. The plans were presented in the form of a little replica of the Palazzo used as a centerpiece for the sumptuous table. Two interior decorators called The Boys, favorites of Horty's from Dallas, exhibited their color schemes—a lot of Fuchsia for Horty loved this favorite color of hers. "You're certainly not going to redecorate that Palazzo" (they said Palazzo the way she did, so that it sounded like "Plotso"), "you're certainly not going to furnish it out of Solomon's Everybody's Store!" The Boys declared to Horty as soon as they heard of her plans to redo the Plotso da Filippo. "Nor," said they, "are you going to make it look like a West Texas ranch house. We're using Florentine silk and Venetian gold, with rosy Fuchsia appointments!"

When Palazzo da Filippo was in shape, the Texas relatives poured in. The Palazzo was crawling with them, young and old. The Palazzo could have been a big Texas house. Black cooks and maids from East Texas mingled with Italian servants. The Venetians loved it. "Viva la Principessa di Texas!" they cried. Those Italianos!

Here I must inform you something of which you were asking about, that on his very wedding night in a villa in Monaco (the beautiful Prince gambled on his wedding night) the beautiful Prince Renzi burst a blood vessel in his inner ear and succumbed (the newspapers' word for it). He just plain died in his wedding bed is what it was. You were asking about how he died. Vicious talk had it that the only stain on the nuptial (newspapers' word)—only stain on the nuptial sheets came from the Prince's ear. Crude. The poor bride, who had been married before—a big textile man from Birmingham, Alabama—was stunned. Poor Horty. Tragedy dogged her, as you well can see. I myself have never experienced the death of a husband but I have experienced two divorces and let me tell you they are simular, they are like a death. They are no fun. My last divorce was particularly nasty. Thank God there was no issue, as the Wills said. Both my husbands were without issue. Issue indeed. That's a joke for the last one, who issued it to *Old Granddad* instead of me—mind as well say it; and excuse the profanity—that one had little issue except through his mouth . . . when he threw up his Bourbon. Crude, I know. But that's mainly the kind of issue *he* had. That ever happen to you? Let's see where was I. Oh. Anyway, this left me in London, quite penniless; tell you why I was in London some other time. Don't have time for that garden path now—it's a memory lane I choose at the moment to take a detour from. But the thing of it is, this is how Horty Solomon got the Palazzo da Filippo, which is what you were asking me about: under the auspices of a sad circumstance—a broken blood vessel leading to death; but a tragedy leading to a new life for her. And for me, as you will soon hear the story (that you were asking about). Anyway, Horty went on with her plans for the Palazzo, now all hers.

As I said somewhere—I can't tell a story straight to save my life, my mind races off onto a hundred things that I remember and want to tell right then, don't want to wait. That ever happen to you? *Anyway,* as I said somewhere, Texans flooded into the canals of Venice because of the Principessa: *Venezia* was half Texas some days—and loved it. And if you've ever heard a Texan speaking Italian, you won't believe the sound of it. Big oilmen came to the Palazzo and Texas college football players—Horty had given them a stadium in Lampasas (they called her Cousin Horty)—Junior League ladies, student concert pianists (Horty was a patron of the Arts, as you will see more about), and once a Rock group—they had that Grand Canal jumping, and some seventeenth-century tiles *fell,* I can tell you. And maybe something from even earlier, a Fresco or two from the Middle Ages. And talented young people who wanted to paint or write came over to the Palazzo. See what Horty did? Some of them were offered rooms in the Palazzo, to write in or paint in, or practice a musical instrument in; and they accepted. See what she did? Palazzo da Filippo jived, that was the word then; it was in the nineteen fifties. That joint jumped, as they said.

I said back there that I was going to tell you why I was in London. Or did I? Can't remember. Just try to remember something with all this noise around here. Italians are noisy, sweet as they are—singing and calling on the Canals. Now where was I? Oh. London. Well, forget London for the time being—*if* I haven't already told it to you. Just keep London in the back of your mind. Now where was I? Oh. Well, you have asked me to tell you what you are hearing—the story of the Texas Principessa, my old schoolmate and life-long pal, that you asked about. After the Prince's death, Horty pulled herself together and got the Palazzo together—a reproduction of Palazzo da Filippo was engraved on Renzi's tombstone *with* Horty's changes incorporated (which, of course, I thought was rather nifty, wouldn't you?)—and Horty pleaded with me in April by phone and cable to come stay. "Come and stay as long as you want to, stay forever if you're happy in the Palazzo; just come on," Horty said, long distance, to me in London. Horty loved to have people in the house. This doesn't mean that she always loved being with them. Sometimes I've seen it happen that a motorboat would arrive and disburse a dozen guests and a week later depart with the same guests and not one of them had ever *seen* the Principessa. Horty would've confined herself off in her own apartment in the far right top wing and there remain in privacy. Simply did not want to have anything to do with them, with her guests. "That's Horty," everyone said. They'd had a grand time, gone in the Principessa's private motorboats to Torcello, to lunch at the Cipriano, to cocktails at other palazzos, been served divine dinners with famous Italians at the da Filippo. But no Horty. She usually—she was so generous—gave expensive presents to her guests to get them to forgive her. Once she gave everybody an egg—a sixth-century—B.C.!—egg of Chinese jade. Amounted to about a dozen eggs. Somebody said the retail value on those eggs was about $150 apiece. Where was I? Oh.

Well this was in April and in May I came. Horty at once announced to me that there was no room for me at the Palazzo! She was getting crazy over painters. She'd become more and more interested in painting, Horty did, but that's no surprise because she always seemed to possess a natural eye and feeling for painting, not so curious for an heiress to generations of garment salesmen, even though you might so comment. For Hortense Solomon inherited good taste and a tendency for her eye to catch fine things when she saw them. Though there were Brahma bulls leering through the windows of the Solomon ranch in West Texas, what those bulls saw inside was fine china and Chippendale, silver and crystal and satin and silk. Those bulls saw the handiwork of a chic decorator and an elegant collector; not every bull sees *that*. So a seventeenth-century palazzo in Venice was not so far a cry for Horty to fix up.

Well here was I living over at the Cipriano where Horty, who couldn't do without me till I got there and then banished me—to a terrific suite, I must say, and footed by her—and here was I coming across the Canal every day to observe the goings on at the Palazzo. Frankly I was glad to have me a little distance from the commotion. Well-known artists came to live in the Palazzo da Filippo and to set up studios there and in the environs. Horty patronized them. Gave them scholarships as she called them. A few were very attractive, I must say, and some very young—Horty's eye again. The Venetians adored La Principessa di Texas. They appreciated her for unscrewing the horse's outfit from the horse sculpture in her garden on the Grand Canal when the Archbishop passed in his barge on days of Holy Procession. The Principessa had commissioned the sculpture of a beautiful horse possessed of some wild spirit, with a head uplifted and long mouth open in an outcry. On it sat a naked man, again possessed of some wild spirit, seemed like, and his mad-looking head was also raised up in some crying out. You did not see the rider's outfit but the horse's was very apparent, and the Principessa commissioned the sculptor—a then unknown but handsome sculptor—to sculpt one that was removable. Which seems to apply to a lot of men that I have known—where was it? A lot of them seem to have removed it. Put it in a drawer someplace. Or mind as well have. Where was I? Oh yes. The horse's outfit. On high holy procession days the Texas Principessa could be seen on her knees under the belly of the horse with grasping hands, making wrenching movements. The Italians coined a phrase for it. When they saw her going at the horse as if she were twisting a light globe, they said to each other that La Principessa di Texas was "honoring the Archbishop." The community generally appreciated her decency for doing this; some felt that the Archbishop should give her a citation. And a few called her a castrator—in Italian of course—*castratazionera,* oh I can't say it right but you know what I mean; and of course a few from home in Texas said she was a dicktwister—had to put their nasty mouths into it. Crude. Where was I. Oh. An American painter came to visit Horty one afternoon. He was showing in the Biennale, which is what they call the show of paintings that they have every year. Horty and the painter drank and talked about his painting. When the Principessa turned around from making *another* double martini for the American painter—she hardly gave it to him when she had to whirl around and make another one—*pirouette* is what you had to do when you made drinks for that man. Unless you just made a whole jug and gave it to him. Anyway, she whirled to find him urinating in the fireplace. The Principessa was so impressed with the American painter—imagine the audacity!—that famous summer afternoon that she asked him to stay. He stayed—over a year, it turned out—and you can see some of his paintings in the palazzo gallery, they have become very sought after and the painter very famous—

though dead from alcoholism not so many years after that. More proof of the ability of discovery that the Principessa had, which is what an article about her recently said. And of the tragic cloud that kept lurking over her life. Even with all her money and the good that she did people, that cloud lurked. And of course it got her, as you well know.

Because Horty's dead. As you well know. Which is what I started out to tell you the details about when you asked me. Well, it was when we were lunching on the terrazzo of the Palazzo. One of those gold June days that Venice has. I'll go right into it and not dwell on it: Horty was bitten by something, some kind of terrible spider, and blood poisoning killed her before we knew it. Guess where the spider was? In a peach. Living at the core of a great big beautiful Italian peach from the sea orchards of the Mediterranean. Horty cried out and fainted. We'd all had a lot of champagne. By the time we got her to the hospital she was dead. Doctor said it was rank poison and that Horty was wildly allergic to it. When she broke the peach open out sprung the horrible black spider. I saw it in a flash. And before she knew it, it had stung her into the bloodstream of her thigh, right through pure silk Italian brocade. I'll never eat a peach again, I'll tell *you*. All Venice was upset. The Archbishop conducted the funeral himself. Horty'd left quite a few *lire* to the Church. We forgot to unscrew the horse's outfit, but when the funeral procession passed by, all the gondoliers took off their hats. Those Italianos!

And I am the new Principessa—except of course I am not a Principessa. But the Italians insist on calling me the new Principessa. The Palazzo is mine. Who ever dreamed that *I* would get the Palazzo? When the will was opened back in Texas they read where Horty had given the place to me! I almost had a heart attack. The will said "to my best friend." But what in the world will I do with a Palazzo, I said. I have not the vast fortune that Horty had. But you have all the paintings of the famous dead American, they said. Sure the family have all fought me for the paintings of the dead American painter. Just let somebody find something good and everybody else tries to get it. Like a bunch of ants. That ever happen to you? They couldn't care less about the Palazzo. But the paintings are something else. The Museum has offered half a million dollars for one. I will not sell yet. And that man that peed in the fire died drunk and broke. Ever hear of such a thing? But they say the pollution is just eating up the paintings. *And* the Palazzo. So far *I'm* safe, but I wonder for how long? And the very town is sinking. Venice is a little lopsided. I don't know where to go. I hardly know how I got here. Sometimes I think who am I where am I? That ever happen to you? But the Texas Principessa is a saint in Venezia. Better not say anything in this town against Horty, I'm telling you. Those Italianos speak her name with reverence and the Archbishop says her name a lot in church. I have offered the horse to the Church, without outfit, but the Archbishop suggested—he's so cute, with a twinkle in his eyes, those *Italianos!*—the Archbishop suggested that *il cavallo* stay where it is. Because it is an affectionate monument for the townspeople, particularly the gondoliers. They point it out to tourists. I hear they're selling little replicas near the Vatican. The sculptor is very upset. He's made many more sculptures (not of horses) but nobody ever paid much attention to any of his other work. Isn't everything crazy? Aren't our lives all crazy? Some days I can't believe any of it. Sometimes I want to go home but I hear Texas is just as crazy. Anyway, that's the story of Horty Solomon da Filippo, the Texas Principessa. Which is what you asked me about, isn't it?

But one more thing. Next morning after the funeral I saw below the terrazzo something sparkling in the dew, something pure silver with diamonds and rubies and emeralds—like something Horty would've worn—and I saw that it was a gorgeous web. And there in the center, all alone, was the horrible black insect that I am sure was the one that had lived at the heart of the peach that killed the Texas Principessa and brought the

Palazzo to me. How could something so ugly and of death make something like that . . . so *beautiful?* I had the oddest feeling, can't describe it. That ever happen to *you?*

Well, that's the story, what you asked me. What happened.

———— ★ ————

A. C. GREENE

———————————————

Before Daylight

The old Chevrolet started cold, sputtered all the way down the inside road and Brian had to race the motor to keep it from dying when they halted for the highway gate. It was still dark as Russ jumped out to pull the barbwire obstruction aside and wait for his dad to drive through so he could close it again. Nobody was on the highway in either direction.

"I've got to get that thermostat fixed or we'll freeze to death this winter," Brian said, as Russ got back in the car and hunched toward the heater.

"You need a new car, Dad," Russ said. "This one was old when I was dating in high school."

"We need a lot of things worse than a new car. Need to keep you in A&M, for one thing. And I've never been ashamed to drive an old car. Some of the farmers round here keep themselves a mile in debt trying to buy a new car or a new pickup every year, but I'll drive anything that will get me to town and back."

The road into Merton was straight, like most roads in West Texas. Even by the Chevrolet's weak headlights, it looked like an invitation to high speed: wide, steep-banked curves and twenty feet of crushed caliche on the shoulders. But now, in the loneliness of early morning, not even a truck was on it.

The car ran all right for an old one, but a heavy bearing knock warned against trying to make it go too fast. The trip into Merton took Brian thirty minutes. By Cadillac it took less than twenty. Most of the farmers and ranchers who used the road made it into town quicker than Brian Holland.

"There's the Holland House," Russ said, feeling rather than seeing the huge, familiar outlines of the old place in the predawn dark. "Remember how I used to draw it all the time? That must have been what started me thinking about being an architect."

"I noticed Ernest was having some kind of a carport put up on the west side when I was by Wednesday," Brian said, without looking toward the house.

"Probably needs some place to keep his RV," Russ said, then laughed. "He doesn't like to have to open the barn doors everytime he gets it out." Russ kept looking at the house. "I see a light in the kitchen. We ought to drop in for a cup of coffee."

"Ernest isn't here now. He's in Denver at the Hereford sale with Champion Domino's Pixie Three."

"Reckon he'll get a hundred thousand for him like he said he would last summer?"

"Probably will. Pixie's a good bull and Top Blanton wants him pretty bad for his herd bull."

Russ looked down the highway. "I met Top Blanton's boy Cress at the Center Springs Stock Show last year. He wasn't showing but he still got most of the attention."

"I imagine he's a lot like Top was. Pretty hard to handle," said Brian.

"Pretty hard to take, you mean. I didn't mention being from Merton. I didn't want to have to go through a lot of name-exchanging about the Hollands, which one I was and who I was kin to."

"Top's boy probably wouldn't know the difference anyway," the father said. "He's never lived here."

"He was driving a Mercedes. A little one. There was a girl with him."

Brian laughed. "Might have been his wife. He's been married three times and he's just now thirty. But don't get envious."

"I'll wait till I'm thirty to get envious."

The heater came on and Brian leaned over to adjust it. "Once it takes hold it can drive you out of the car." He straightened up and said, "I know you've been over there to see her while you've been home . . . are you still serious about La Nelle Lloyd?"

"Not really. It's just something left over from high school." Russ paused. "She'll find her a husband down in Austin. This is just her second year at the university. La Nelle's too good-looking to wait on an old high school sweetheart."

"Do you care?" Brian asked.

Russ thought again. "I guess not. She'll marry somebody rich as she is. I just hope it's not Hardy. I don't know that I'd like to see her married to my cousin."

"She and Hardy seeing one another now? I hadn't heard that."

"Down at the university. I think her sorority sisters expect it of her—she's from Merton then she wants to be dating Ernie Holland's son."

"Is Ernest that well-known at the University of Texas?"

"Uncle Ernie's one of the richest men in the state, Dad. First thing people at school ask, when they find out I'm from Merton, is if I'm kin to Ernie Holland. He's a big A&M giver, even if he never went to college."

"Well, this time next year you'll have your license and be set up with some firm in Houston or Dallas and can forget about La Nelle and Hardy. And Ernest. By the way, Ernest said that Japanese fellow that lectured at A&M last fall thought a lot of your work."

"Watanabe . . . yeah, he was pretty nice, but he's too high-powered. If I was at MIT, maybe . . . but he was just being pleasant."

"Ernest seemed to think he was serious."

"He might have been . . . I guess he was. But, you know, his interns, associates, don't make a whole lot when they're first working with him. I can't afford the honor."

"Why did you tell Ernest about it and not me?"

"Uncle Ernie asked *me* about it. He had talked with somebody at school."

"You could have mentioned it to your father. I'm the one's keeping you there. And when did you see Ernest? He hasn't been here since you've been home."

"He was on campus. Down at school. Took me across the river for a beer."

"I resent my brother trying to take you over. He's got a boy. He's always wanting to run things. When Papa died, he tried to step in and make all my decisions for me, and Mama always sided with him."

"But, Dad . . . he's so much older than you. He's what, twelve years? He had to take over. You were just a kid."

"He held it against me when I went on my own instead of with him."

Russ laughed, "Maybe you should have . . . Uncle Ernie's done pretty well for himself."

"You don't have any cause for complaint; Ernest Holland wasn't the one that kept you in high school and sent you to college."

"I was just joking, Dad. I've never compared you to Uncle Ernie."

The road dipped into a gentle valley. South, a line of lights marked the rigs of the Kline oilfield. A lighted sign with a big red arrow pointed down a gravel road that led to the field. As Brian and Russ passed, a pipe truck was waiting to pull onto the highway.

"They've brought in two more wells on Dad Kline's place since October," Brian said.

"Mother wrote me first thing that she was getting a little royalty out of it now," Russ said.

"That's the one-sixteenth her mother left her over by Hidden Valley. They've already drilled as many wells around it as the Railroad Commission will allow."

"Mother's pretty proud of that royalty check, isn't she?"

"Mostly because it's made out to Mildred Kline Holland and not Mrs. Brian Holland," the father said.

"What would mother do if she wasn't a Kline?" Russ smiled as he said it.

"She might not mind being a Holland if she was the right Holland," Brian said, then added, "Let's not talk about the Hollands any more. I'm sick of the subject. Any of the teachers ever say anything about me to you?"

"Dr. Gentry does. He said he was surprised I was studying architecture when the Hollands have always been ranch people. I told him I wanted to build a new house of Holland."

"What did he say to that?"

"He just laughed. He could see it was a joke."

"Scott Gentry spent a lot of time in the old house when he was trying to marry your aunt Ella. He came out to do animal husbandry research, he claimed—but it was mainly to be around Ella. I had to share my bedroom with him because I was the youngest one in the family."

"Who built that house? Your father?" Russ asked.

"Papa didn't build it. He just added the front section," Brian said. "My great-grandfather built the main part in 1880, before the railroad came through or there was a Merton."

"Who put the lightning rods up? I've always loved the way those lightning rods stick out of every gable and ridge on the place."

"I don't know who put up the lightning rods. It was before my time. Ernest had that big satellite dish mounted on his antenna last fall so he could get all the Dallas Cowboy and Houston Oiler games."

"I wish there had been some way *we* could have got the Holland House," Russ said.

"Well, I've got to be fair to Ernest, in this instance. He took care of Mama and she lived in the house 'til she died. He deserved it. Mama was pretty costly. She wouldn't live like a widow, except a rich one. I guess I could have had it if I'd been able to support her, but it was out of the question."

Dawn was just turning the eastern edge of the horizon pink as they rounded a long, wide curve into the outskirts of Merton. A subdivision under construction looked like a flock of treeless turkeys in the gray light.

"They've built out almost to the Hog Hole," Brian said, looking at the line of trees which marked the course of Bog Wagon Creek. "I learned to swim in the Hog Hole the summer I worked in town with Tommy Evans and courted your mother."

"I learned to swim in Uncle Ernie's pool," Russ said.

"They've named this 'Belgrade Heights,' as if anybody in Merton knows what or where Belgrade is. I don't like it. I personally think Bog Wagon would have been pretty colorful, or at least Madero Heights, after the old Juan Madero survey most of this land's on. But, no, this bunch doesn't know anything about history, or care."

Merton was just coming awake as the old car went down Haskell Boulevard. South Milam, which was the U.S. highway, carried about a dozen cars. At the bus station they parked around the corner. A dozen persons were already waiting for the Dallas-bound bus.

Russ carried his bag and a drawing board. The waiting room was quiet, with the travelers looking anxious to get going and the ones who brought them down looking sleepy and loosely dressed. While Russ went to check his bag, Brian thought how he used to know all the Merton passengers any-time he went to the bus station, or the train station when the railroad still had passenger service. Now it was another town altogether.

Brian remembered when the bus station was also the ter-minal for the army camp buses during World War II, and how eager he had been for the war to last long enough for him to go, after Ernest had been drafted. Soldiers had lined up by the thousands to catch the bus on Sunday nights, with queues stretching two blocks down Santa Fe Street, which ran to the west of the old bus station. The camp buses ran every three or four minutes at such times, sometimes all night long. It had looked glamorous to him, a little country boy.

Russ came back with his baggage check.

"Bus will be here in eleven minutes," he said. "They're running two sections, so I might get a seat into Dallas. Some-times it's pretty crowded."

"Don't you wish you could afford to fly?"

Russ grinned. "I feel more at home on a Trailways bus."

"Is there an airline that flies into College Station?" Brian asked.

"Yeah, there is. A little one. But most of the kids have cars. I guess I could have gotten a ride with Joe Flynn if I'd thought about it. He's from Merton. Maybe I will next time."

Russ looked at his father, uncertainty on his face. "Dad, I've been putting off telling you, I guess, but Uncle Ernie's of-fered me a job. With him. A damn good job, better than I could get anywhere, regardless."

"What kind of job can he offer you? He doesn't need an architect."

"He's going to . . . I mean, he's going to start developing

95

industrial parks and office complexes all over the south and west. It's big stuff. Exciting."

"But you couldn't handle that kind of work . . . not without a lot of experience. You ought to go ahead and go on your own, then, by God, let him hire you because you're good, not because you're kin to him."

"Well, it's not even that, Dad. It's more than just doing planning. He wants me to be his manager; start out working in planning but later on to run the whole thing. He says I'm too valuable to let go of."

"What about his own son? Why can't Hardy take over and be valuable?"

"Dad . . . you know Hardy. Hardy's not interested. He's not going to get interested; he's older than I am. Uncle Ernie's set up a big trust fund for Hardy. He can do anything he wants. That's the first thing I asked Uncle Ernie, was what about Hardy. He says he'll put it all in writing, that Hardy's the last person I need to worry about. You're the one."

"He thinks I'm the one, does he? Well, damn right, he better worry about me; trying to take my son away from me. Still trying to control my life. He'd better worry about me."

"Dad . . . he didn't say *he* needed to worry about you. He said *I* did."

Brian's face collapsed, "You don't believe that."

Russ said softly, "Of course I don't. So I've already accepted the job."

"You've taken the job? Didn't even mention it the whole time you've been home?"

"I never could find the right time."

"You were afraid, weren't you?"

"A little bit. I know how you've . . . felt . . . about Uncle Ernie."

Brian started to say something, then shook his head. "No you don't. It's not how I've felt about Ernest. It's how I've felt about myself. I'm not jealous, but all my life, all my damn life,

Ernest won . . . and I lost. Ernest was the big brother, I was the baby. Ernest played football, I sang in the choir. Ernest went to war and mother wrote him every night; I went to college and nobody even saw me off at the train station—except Ernest. Ernest married big old Sally Lukes from the wrong side of the tracks, and she inherited ten thousand acres of desert with oil under every acre. I quit school to marry pretty little Mildred Kline, and she gets a $325-a-month royalty check from the Kline field. Ernest never finished high school but A&M named a library for him; I'm a dirt farmer, a tractor seat philosopher with Henry James in the bookcase and a twelve-year-old Chevy in the garage. The only time I won was you. And now he gets you."

Hard, reluctant tears were on the father's cheeks, although he tried to hide them and wipe them off. The silver nose of the bus loomed in the plate glass window across the front of the station and the waiting room crowd quickly pulled itself to its feet, and spread through the front door out to the bus.

"Dad . . . it's not that way; not that way at all, any of it."

The two men quickly embraced, the boy hesitating to turn loose of his father, who pushed him, almost roughly, toward the bus. "Go on and get a seat. It looks crowded." Russ reached toward him, "Dad!" but the older man was retreating toward the station's side door. He turned, no longer trying to hide the wetness of his face. "We'll see you in June," he said.

Good Rockin' Tonight

The year Elvis died was a strange year, and I remember it not only because of what happened to my brother, Bubba, but because that was the year we had our first transsexual here in Nortex. Bobby Joe Pitts, who worked for Builders' Supply, told the wife and kids he still loved them, but he couldn't stand it any longer: He'd always felt like a woman in a man's body and wanted to go to Houston for a sex-change operation.

He'd been saving money for years in a secret account and was all ready to go through with it. But the doctor in Houston was cautious. He told Bobby Joe he should try wearing women's clothes for six months before the operation, since there would be no going back. So Bobby Joe came to our church, First Methodist, looking something like Mary Tyler Moore. His family took it hard. The preacher suggested, after the services, that he go to the Unitarian church instead, where they took homosexuals and drug addicts. Bobby Joe stormed out, saying we were hypocrites and had no spirit of Christian love.

The first nice day rolled around, he was out at Skyline Country Club, just like every other year, for his eighteen holes of Saturday morning golf. Harley Otis told me when I walked into the locker room. Said Bobby Joe expected to play in the club tournament, but against the women. Harley was disgusted. "I guess it had to happen here," he said, snorting and throwing his shoes all the way across the room, where they hit the big picture of Arnold Palmer on the locker room wall.

I felt sorry for Bobby Joe and went out to where he was teeing off alone. He said he was no different from that doctor who became a lady tennis pro. "They're just threatened," he said primly. About that time, Harley drove past in his electric cart and shouted out, asking Bobby Joe if he was for the ERA. Bobby Joe shot him the finger.

That night I sat on my patio, drinking Jack Daniel's and looking up at the stars. Through the sliding glass doors, I could see my wife watching her favorite program. Hell, I could see Bobby Joe's point of view. I might like being a woman myself if I looked like Mary Tyler Moore. Trouble was, I wouldn't; and neither would Bobby Joe. I doubted any amount of plastic surgery could do the trick. My wife, alone there in the den, laughed at something on television, and I felt like a ghost. I decided the world was changing so fast nobody could keep up with it.

I'm a doctor myself, obstetrics and gynecology, and I've got a little office across the street from the hospital. Who should come see me the next day but my old high school sweetheart, Nadine MacAfee, whom I'd seen no more than two or three times in all the years since graduation. But my heart still stopped when I saw her there in the reception room.

In my office, she told me she'd like to get off the pill and try some other form of contraception. She dropped hints about her loneliness and talked nostalgically about the days when we'd gone steady; and I soon realized she was looking for romance. I was so nervous I thought I was going to stammer for the first time in years, and resorted to a trick the speech therapist had taught me: flipping my pencil up and catching it, not thinking too much about what I was saying.

"Look, Nadine," I said finally, "if it's all the same, I'd rather not examine you. But I can recommend another doctor."

"That's all right, Ross," she said. "I understand."

She had once been so shy, and this was a pretty bold thing for her to do. But I had never gone all the way with Nadine in high school and I wasn't about to now. I wanted to keep her the way she was in my memory—full of innocence and mystery. So I took out the bottle I keep in my desk drawer, we had a drink, and I got her talking about her kids, my pencil flipping just like old Johnny Carson's.

When I showed her out, my brother, Bubba, who was a big wheel with the Prudential Insurance Company, was sitting in the reception room with a long face on. When I asked him what was wrong, he told me Elvis had died and we had to celebrate his passing away. "The King is gone," he said, "and nobody will ever replace him." I sent the rest of my patients home.

I hadn't known Elvis was so important to my brother, but then I really didn't know Bubba anymore. We played golf now and then, but our wives hated each other, which seems to be the rule, not the exception; so we never saw each other socially, not at all.

We drove out to a bar in the new shopping mall, where neither of us had ever been. Thank God It's Friday's it was called, and I think it was supposed to look like Greenwich Village.

"What the hell has happened here?" my brother said.

"How do you mean, Bubba?"

"What's happened to this town? Why is everyone pretending they're in New York City?"

"I don't know, Bubba; I guess it's television."

To me, the whole shopping mall was a depressing place. Nobody had been able to rest until we got one, just like every other town. There must have been a thousand editorials in the paper about it. On the way in, we'd passed droves of sad-looking teenagers hanging out around the fountain, and I'd thought how much happier we looked out at the Pioneer Drive-In, in our cars. But everyone was proud of the mall as they could be, and who was wrong, them or me?

Harley Otis was there, right in the thick of it, wearing polyester pants, white loafers with gold chains, a leather jacket, and a Dacron shirt with the collar spread out on his shoulders. There was also a little gold chain around his neck.

"Who you tryin' to look like, Harley?" my brother asked. "The Six Million Dollar Man?"

Harley took it as a compliment and started telling us how he'd just gotten back from a Successful Life course in Dallas where he'd learned the importance of a Positive Mental Attitude. "You've got to set goals for yourself," he said.

"What's your goal, Harley?"

"Right now, I'm buckin' for president of Kiwanis. But my immediate goal is to get into Tina Eubank's pants."

I looked over and there was Tina, twice divorced, standing by the jukebox. It didn't look like he'd have too much trouble. "Y'all have a nice day," Harley said, and slid toward her.

Then we drove out the Fort Worth Highway, my brother talking about everything he hated, from women's lib to *People* magazine. I hadn't seen him like this for years. There had been a time, when I was in med school and my brother was driving a truck, when he developed all sorts of theories about why this country was going to pieces. He also claimed to have seen UFOs and talked to them on his CB. I finally diagnosed the problem when I discovered he was taking "L.A. turnarounds"—those biphetamine capsules truckers use on long hauls. Once he started working for the Prudential, he settled down and that side of him disappeared.

But now he was driving too fast and talking crazy, like he used to; looking around at everything and not liking what he saw. Just then, I heard a siren and saw flashing blue lights, and a highway patrol car pulled us over.

It was Floyd Simms, whom I hadn't seen in maybe fifteen years. "Could I see your operator's license?" he asked, all business, holding his metal clipboard.

"It's Bubba Moody, Floyd."

"You were exceeding a posted speed limit of fifty-five miles per hour, and it looks to me like you got alcoholic beverages in the car."

"Floyd, don't you remember? We took shop together."

"Yeah, I remember. But shitfire, Bubba, you were driving like a bat."

"Floyd, Elvis died today."

"I heard."

"My brother and I are drinking to his memory. Don't give me the cold shoulder, Floyd. Have a drink with us and let's remember all the good and bad old days."

"Well, I do get off duty in half an hour," Floyd said, looking across the car at me and grinning. "That really you, Ross?"

Then the three of us went out to the old colored man's place. It was my brother's idea. You could have knocked me over with a stick when I saw it was still there, the little redbrick building with the sign that said HOT PIT COOKED BAR-B-QUE.

The old man himself, who had a big stomach and a pencil mustache (Fats Domino, we had called him), opened the counterweighted lid of the stove. Inside was at least a chine of beef. He cut off slabs and put them on bread. Then he added half a green onion and a wedge of longhorn cheese and wrapped it all in butcher paper.

We carried our sandwiches to a table, and the other customers, all colored (black, I corrected myself), sort of looked at
us without looking at us, for Floyd still wore his highway patrol
uniform; then got up and left, dropping their trash in the
garbage can on the way out.

"See, big brother?" Bubba said. "The past is still here, all
around us."

I couldn't take my eyes off my sandwich. It sat there on
the tabletop, which was bare except for a Louisiana Hot Sauce
bottle full of toothpicks. Grease spotted the butcher paper. I
took a bite and it ran down my chin. Lord, it was good.

Bubba returned from the cooler with three bottles of
Royal Crown Cola, the old-style bottles with the yellow pyra-
mids on them. "Look at that," he said softly, staring at his bottle. "Would you look at that?" Then he drank it.

"What are you up for, Floyd?" he said.

"My wife's going to be wondering where I am," Floyd
said, and when Bubba gave him a sour look, added, "Shitfire, Bubba, there's a good program on tonight. About Vince
Lombardi."

I nodded. "My wife's not home. Tonight's her yoga class.
Y'all could come over and watch it." What was I saying "y'all"
for? I hadn't said "y'all" in years.

"What's so important about Vince Lombardi?" Bubba
said. "You never knew him. A night like this comes once in a
lifetime, and tonight the three of us are going to the Cotton
Bowling Palace."

So we drove on down to the long, low building on Holiday Creek, full of the odor of paste wax and the thunder of
balls; and the same people were there who had always been
there, roughnecks and refinery workers and railroad brakemen.
I was clumsy at first, dropping the ball on the lane with a thud;
but Bubba was greasing them in right off. We didn't bother to
keep score. None of us could remember how. We just bowled,
and I relaxed, for by now the evening was lost, anyway, watch-

ing Bubba cut up, bowling like Don Carter, and so forth. He could always impersonate anyone he wanted. Mom said his version of me was deadly. When he came over and dropped down beside me in one of the green plastic chairs, I felt a stab of brotherhood and socked him on the arm, the way I would have in the old days.

"Hey, Bubba," I said. "You old son of a bitch."

"You're not sorry you're not home watching the life of old Vince Lombardi?"

"No, Bubba. I genuinely enjoyed this night."

"Life is a road."

"Yes, Bubba. Life is a road." I waited for him to finish, so drunk the bowling balls sounded like they were rolling through my head.

"Once I thought I knew who I was and where I was going. I could see the road ahead. But I lost my way."

Floyd was out on the lane, yelling. A pin had fallen outside the gate, and when nobody appeared to help, he walked up the lane, slipping and falling down, and got it himself. People were laughing at him.

"There was only one person of our time who never stopped. Who became the person he dreamed of becoming."

"Who's that?"

"Elvis," my brother said.

Do you know what he did then? He stepped up to the booth where you got your shoes and where they called your number when your lane was ready. He grabbed the microphone away from the fat lady who was sitting there and sang "Love Me Tender" to her. It started as a joke, but this was the day Elvis had died, and when he finished, the place was dead quiet. Then everyone applauded and started shouting, "More, more," and I was shouting, too. And he did sound exactly like Elvis, although I never thought he looked like him at all. I thought he looked more like Conway Twitty.

*   *   *

One year later to the day, I was riding down Highway 82 in a white Cadillac Eldorado. The oil-well pumping jacks nodded in the fields, the blacktop shimmered in the heat, and in the front seat was my brother Bubba, wearing a white jump suit with silver studs, his hair dyed black. The sign on the side of the car read:

EL TEX AS

BUBBA MOODY KING OF ROCK AND ROLL

NORTEX' OWN ELVIS

Floyd Simms was driving, wearing Las Vegas shades and the Robert Hall suit Bubba had bought him at the Hub Clothing Store.

Bubba had done better than I would have believed, perfecting his act at Kiwanis and Rotary dances. He'd also done benefits for the crippled and retarded children, which people liked, and borrowed enough money to lease this Eldorado just like the one Elvis had. Now we were on our way to the first stop on Bubba's summer tour, which was to end at Six Flags Over Texas. There was to be a convention of Elvis Presley impersonators, and Bubba intended to prove he was the best in the world.

"This is the life, isn't it?" he said, looking back at me and grinning. "Man, sometimes I feel so good I've got to go out and take a walk through K-Mart to bring myself down."

We stopped at the Cow Lot in Nocona, where Bubba bought a pair of ostrich-hide boots and gave the owner an eight-by-ten autographed glossy photo, which he thumbtacked on the wall next to the photos of Willie Nelson, Arthur Godfrey, Howard Hughes, and all the other celebrities who, down through the years, had bought Nocona boots.

When we got back in the car, Bubba said, "Floyd, I think

I'm going to ask you to dye your hair red so I can call you Red West." That was Elvis's bodyguard. Bubba really wanted to make the act authentic.

We came to a billboard that said we were eight miles from Decatur, home of Dico Sausage, and showed a pair of rolling dice. "Pull over, Floyd," Bubba said.

He struck a karate pose in front of the billboard and Floyd took his picture with the Polaroid Swinger. I was getting back in the car when I heard a buzz just like an electric alarm clock going off.

"Christ, Bubba, what the hell you doing?" Floyd said. Bubba had picked up a baby rattlesnake out of the ditch and was making like he was going to kiss it, holding it inches away from his lips.

"Get a picture, get a picture," he shouted, laughing like an idiot.

We drove on through more North Texas and finally into Decatur, where a banner across the street proclaimed Bubba's show. "The King is here," my brother said.

Floyd parked and we walked into the high school, across the street from the red-granite courthouse. The band was already setting up. Down in the dressing room, Bubba put on his makeup and I sat on a box of textbooks in the corner and watched. Already you could hear people filling the auditorium upstairs. "Sounds like a good crowd," Bubba said, gluing on his fake sideburns.

Then a local disc jockey appeared with a tape recorder and Miss Billie Tucker, president of Bubba's North Texas fan club. She'd brought along a list she'd compiled of characteristics Bubba and Elvis had in common. The disc jockey held up his microphone and she read it, perspiration on her upper lip.

"Both Elvis and Bubba are Capricorns," she said. "Both were truck drivers, both stationed with the army in Germany, and both were devoted to their mothers. Both are overweight,

107

both like Cadillac Eldorados, and both like to stay up all night. Both have fantastic sex appeal . . ."

Good Lord, I thought. These people are serious.

Upstairs, I found myself in an ordinary high school auditorium. There were flags of the United States and Texas on either side of the stage. The ceiling was high, yellowish globes shedding a dim light. Probably the Pledge of Allegiance had been said here thousands of times. Tonight it was full of more middle-aged women than I'd ever seen in one place, and the clicking of high heels and pocketbooks was a constant roar.

Then the house lights went down and it got dead silent. The curtain rose in the darkness and a spotlight stabbed down and my brother leaped into it. He tore into "Heartbreak Hotel" like a man possessed. My brother, who had been good, had gotten better. Maybe he really was the best. He had all the moves down, and from this distance it made no difference at all that he wasn't a carbon copy of Elvis.

He sang "Blue Suede Shoes" and "Don't Be Cruel" and "Jailhouse Rock" and spoke of the series of miracles that had brought Elvis to the top in so short a time. He said Elvis had loved black music and made a plea for integration and sang "In the Ghetto." All this time, he was throwing scarves into the audience and women were fighting for them. Then he said, "There's been a great loss of faith in this country. Maybe it was Nixon, maybe Vietnam. I voted for Nixon, but he betrayed us. He thought he could get away with fooling us rednecks." He looked around, his face incandescent in the spotlight. "That's right. I'm a redneck. So are you. And so was Elvis. We're the people who kept the faith."

There was more, but I don't really remember all he said; and he didn't write it down, he spoke right from the heart. He asked for a moment of silence for the boys who had died in Vietnam, and sang "How Great Thou Art." Then he ripped right into "Hound Dog" and disappeared without an encore.

The lights came up and we were back in that shabby little auditorium with flags on either side of the stage.

The audience went wild, like they'd just woke up, and I ran downstairs to Bubba's dressing room, where you could hear them stomping on the floor overhead.

Then Floyd said, "Here come the autograph hounds," and opened the door and they poured in. Bubba signed his own glossies as fast as they could shove them at him, and pretty soon a woman grabbed his gold chain and tore it right off his neck.

"We'd better get out of here, Bubba," Floyd said, and we shoved through the crowd. But they had our way blocked and we had to detour into the girls' rest room. Bubba was still laughing, but to tell the truth I was scared. We climbed out the window and ran across the parking lot, where someone from the band was waiting in the Eldorado. We all piled in and drove off, a crowd of women following us all the way to the corner.

"They shoulda had cops there," Bubba said after a while. "I told them we'd need cops. Floyd, you'd better start packing a rod. You're gonna need it if there's any more crowd scenes like this."

At Six Flags, Bubba demolished the other Elvis impersonators. What surprised me was how many there were. They came in all shapes and sizes, and one had come from as far away as Nebraska. There was only one who was serious competition: Claude Thibodeaux, from New Iberia, Louisiana, who billed himself as the Cajun Elvis. He had flash, but nobody could beat Bubba for sheer impact.

Right after his performance, Bubba was approached by someone who wanted to manage him. Elvis Presley's manager, as everyone knows, was Colonel Tom Parker. This was Bud Parker, late a colonel in the U.S. Air Force. The coincidence tickled them both. He promised Bubba in one year he'd be playing Caesar's Palace in Las Vegas.

I was packing my suitcase when Bubba came into my room and said, "Big brother, you and me are going to Houston."

"What for?"

"Looka here at this telegram."

The telegram was from Nancy Jo Miller, who'd been Bubba's high school love. She was married now and lived in Houston. She said she'd read about his act, congratulated him, and hoped they could get together sometime.

Sometimes my brother dumbfounded me. But I couldn't say no, and anyway, he was paying for the tickets. So instead of going home, we flew to Houston on Trans Texas, got a rented car and a room at the Holiday Inn.

Nancy Jo lived in a $200,000 brick colonial on the edge of Houston, with pine trees growing in the front yard. Bubba had this idea he wanted to drop in and surprise her, so we didn't phone ahead. He slipped on his shades and I rang the doorbell. I felt sorry for Bubba: He was as nervous as a kid on his first date.

Just for a moment I saw Nancy Jo as she really was, a little faded around the eyes and mouth. But the years had been good to her. I suppose you could say she resembled Angie Dickinson—which, in a way, was a hell of a lot better than she'd looked in high school.

"Oh, my Lord," she said, when she saw Bubba in his white Elvis jump suit, and gave a short, embarrassed laugh that was cut off as if by a knife. Then she said, "I'll make y'all bloody marys," and disappeared into the kitchen.

"This was a mistake," Bubba said. He was trembling so hard I had to hold him up.

Nancy Jo came back and we sat in the tiny front room with the big picture window, which I knew was almost never used except for guests. What with the baby grand piano and the big sofa and the glass-topped coffee table, there was hardly room for the three of us; but from the first, I don't even think they knew I was there. They were totally absorbed in each other.

She poured out the story of all that had happened since they'd seen each other last, and I stared at the celery stalk in my bloody mary and tried not to listen.

Nancy Jo had intended to marry Bubba, but he had to do his army service, and there seemed to be all the time in the world; so she went to Dallas and enrolled in stewardess school. She pictured herself wearing that cute uniform and doing favors for the passengers, bringing them pillows and playing with their kids.

She lived with some other stews on Gaston Avenue, and there were some pretty wild parties; but Nancy Jo locked herself in her room and did crossword puzzles and wrote love letters to Bubba.

It was the airplane that did her in. The other stews hung out in the galley, where you could meet pro football players and rich oilmen. Nancy Jo didn't want a rich oilman: She was going to have Bubba. So she fought it.

But the airplane was the most boring place in the world. The kids were snotty and their parents were cross and didn't appreciate the favors you did for them. There was nothing to do but look out the window, and when you did, what did you see? Clouds.

In the end, she went to the galley, which was like a nickel-plated singles bar, so tiny you couldn't turn around without bumping into some horny guy. There she met Calvin Sloate, a corporate lawyer for Texaco; and they drank Scotch out of tiny bottles while the galley roared like a sea shell, rocking slightly in the rough air 20,000 feet over Indianapolis.

"I'm sorry, Bubba," she said. "But you were going to be in the army for another year and that seemed like forever. I had to get off that airplane." So she had married Calvin, and now seventeen years had flashed by like nothing at all.

"We've got a condo in Vero," she said, "and one in Aspen, and last year we went skiing at Sundance and Lisa had her picture taken with Robert Redford."

"Lisa?" Bubba asked in a flat voice.

"My daughter," she said, showing us another picture. "That's her with her Arabian stallion. She loves horses."

She showed us the rest of the house. We stood for a moment at the door of Calvin's study, like visitors at a museum looking into one of those rooms closed off with a velvet rope. Calvin had a collection of beer cans, one from every country in the world; a pair of expensive shotguns; and a lampshade made of *Playboy* centerfolds. I had already noticed his radar-equipped bass boat in the driveway.

In the bedroom, she slid back the closet door and showed us her $500 Italian shoes. Bubba just looked at her and said, "You know you broke my heart, don't you?"

"Oh, Bubba, don't say that. It sounds so horrible. And, anyway, how could I know you cared that much? Look here."

She took from under her costly shoes the old high school yearbook; and there, on the same page, were their pictures. Their faces were soft and unformed but shining with a sort of light. Bubba had a flattop with "fenders"—long on the sides and short on the top. Over his face he had written, in blue ball-point pen: "Had a lot of good times with you and hope to see more of you next year. Bubba."

"Couldn't you have said more than that?" she asked, tears in her eyes. "How was I to know I was so important to you?"

"In those days," Bubba said, "you won the game of love by pretending you didn't care. Yeah, that's all we thought love was, a game. But it turned out to be a more serious game than we thought."

At this point I left the room, phoned a cab, and went back to the Holiday Inn. I don't think they missed me. It rained, and there I spent the rest of the afternoon watching *Return to Earth,* a TV movie about the life of an astronaut, and drinking Jack Daniel's. Later, Bubba came back. "Well, big brother," he said, "it's all settled. She's leaving her husband and I'm leaving my wife, and everything's going to be like it was." He'd been walking around in the rain and his clothes were soaked.

But I was skeptical that Bubba could so easily turn back the clock. Now that he'd become a star, he thought anything was possible. To me, he was like that astronaut who'd achieved his boyhood dream and went to the moon; but sooner or later, he had to come back down to earth and be an ordinary person like the rest of us. On the plane home, Bubba turned to me and said, "Big Brother, I'm going to tell you something. You're the only one who'll understand."

"Yes, Bubba?"

"My whole life, I've felt like I was in the wrong body or something. But when I'm Elvis . . . I got it right. I'm the person I should have been, the person I've always known I could be."

Now it struck me that this was what Bobby Joe Pitts, the would-be transsexual, had said. Like Bubba, he only felt like himself when he was somebody else.

"Do you know what I'm saying?" Bubba whispered, holding my shoulder in an iron grip.

Yes, I knew. At the best moments of my life—when I hit a good golf shot or had a woman I adored—I felt like someone else. A version of me, maybe, but a version that was to Ross Moody what a Cadillac Eldorado was to a Ford Pinto. I doubted you could totally become that perfect version of yourself. Bubba felt that way now, but he could not be El Tex As for the rest of his life.

But that was the happiest I ever saw Bubba. On this flight, we had, instead of a stewardess, a male flight attendant. Ordinarily, Bubba would have made some sarcastic comment; but on that day, he seemed at peace with himself. I slept most of the way, but once I woke up. Bubba, in the hollow roar of the cabin, was looking through the porthole and smiling down at the dark world below.

* * *

When he broke the news to his wife, Jan, she knew just how to take it: like Jill Clayburgh in that movie about the New York woman, nodding, her eyes closed, finishing his sentences for him.

"And so," he said, "I am going to—"

"Move out. All right, buster, go ahead. Do yourself a big favor."

They were standing in the den, and she poked through the big glass bowl on top of the television set full of matchbooks from every restaurant they'd ever been to.

"You'd just better get yourself a good lawyer," she told him.

The strange thing, he said, was that she seemed almost glad. Here it was, the crisis predicted so often. Now she would learn to think for herself and be happy (like Rhoda once she got rid of that slob, Joe), maybe even write a book. The possibilities were endless.

"There is one more thing," Bubba said. "Here is a list of our close friends whom I do not want you to sleep with, as they would be laughing at me behind my back."

"Thank you," she said. "I know just what to do with it."

She slept with the first one, Bubba's boss at the Prudential, that very night; and spent the rest of the week working her way down the list.

Nancy Jo also left Calvin Sloate but, on the advice of a girlfriend, went to a therapist, and the first thing he did was tell her not to make any more sudden moves.

She phoned Bubba and said, "I'm living in an apartment complex with plastic ivy on the walls. There's nobody here but kids; and my lawyer says I won't get any kind of settlement, since I moved out. Bubba, I'm having second thoughts."

So Bubba sped down to Houston, even though he was starting another tour in a few days. Nancy Jo wouldn't see him right away: She had to look through her appointment book and set a date. When they finally got together, all she would do was talk for hours. She had a whole new vocabulary and she wouldn't drink bloody marys anymore, just white wine and something called Amaretto, which Bubba said tasted like Log Cabin syrup.

She was changing, slipping away; but Bubba was desperate to prove he could accept her under any conditions. He went to see her therapist himself and even took her to a Woody Allen movie.

I didn't see Bubba for months. At the end of his tour, he phoned from Abilene and asked if I'd come down. I found him that night at the Cross Plains Motel, a real dump.

His appearance shocked me: He'd gained maybe forty pounds. He said, "Did you bring your little black bag?"

"Yeah. What for?"

"You got any speed in it?"

I was offended and told him to forget it. He said it was hard for him to keep his weight down, being on the road and all and eating nothing but junk food. But I wouldn't be talked into it. Then I went right into the john and flushed all my pills down the toilet.

When I came back out, Bubba was talking to Floyd, who had his hair dyed red. I sat down and noticed my chair had a Rocking R brand on the arm. It was Roy Rogers furniture, probably bought for some kid thirty years ago, and it had ended up here in this terrible motel. For the first time, I glimpsed the sadness singers talk about of being on the road, and thought it was getting to Bubba.

Floyd said he had a girl for Bubba. "Tell her I'll meet her in one hour," Bubba said. "The usual conditions."

The conditions under which Bubba met his fans were these: They had to be between the ages of thirty-five and forty-five, they had to provide their own car, and they had to park on a dirt road on the edge of town. When Bubba appeared in the Eldorado, they flashed their lights if it was safe. Then

Bubba parked and came ahead on foot, bringing his own bottle.

I thought this was a foolish, adolescent thing to do, and told him so.

"You know, big brother," he said, "I feel sorry for you. You been fooling around with women's private parts for so long you've forgotten what they're for."

Like everything Bubba said, there was some truth to this. In my years as a gynecologist, I'd examined most of the girls I'd worshipped in high school, and it meant less than nothing to me. It made me wonder about my choice of profession.

"When are you playing Las Vegas?" I asked him.

"Colonel Parker says I'm not ready for Vegas. I need one more thing to put me over the top—plastic surgery, so I'm identical to Elvis. 'Course, there'll be no goin' back—but it's worth it if it gets me to Caesar's Palace."

"No," I said. "No, Bubba. You can't do that."

"Why not?"

I couldn't exactly say, but I was thinking: If he loses his face, he loses himself.

"Bobby Joe Pitts decided not to," I said.

"Bobby Joe Pitts?"

"You know. The plastic surgeon told him he should try living like a woman. Well he joined a women's group, and now he's changed his mind. He says he thought men were boring, but women have the most boring conversations in the world."

This got my brother furious. "Are you comparing me to some miserable little pervert? Christ, Bobby Joe . . . why, he wore a brassiere under his football jersey the whole senior year. And we thought he was joking!"

"Will Nancy Jo love you if you don't have your own face?"

He took a pistol out of the desk drawer, a Colt Python, and spun it around his finger and said, "Nancy Jo doesn't know what she wants. Last time I talked to her, she said she wanted space. I said, 'Hell, you can have all the space you want, once we're married.'" He aimed the pistol at the television screen, where Elvis was singing to Ann-Margret. It was a reshowing of *Viva Las Vegas* on cable TV.

"His voice sorta went to pieces, didn't it?" Bubba said. "Frankly, I think I'm better now than he ever was."

"Bubba, put down that gun."

"Come on," he said. "I'm going to get some nooky."

So Floyd drove us out to the edge of town, where we parked on a dirt road and could see ahead, dimly, the outline of another car.

"She's not flashing her lights," Floyd said. "It must not be safe yet."

I rolled down the window. There was a full moon that night and I thought I could hear the distant yip of coyotes.

When I mentioned it, Floyd said, "Ain't no more coyotes in this county. Farmers wiped them out with traps and poisoned bait."

Still, I thought I could hear them, as I had on so many nights when we'd driven out on Red River Road.

"Do you have to do this, Bubba? What about Nancy Jo?"

"A man's got to get his satisfaction. And if you can't be near the one you love, love the one you're near."

The headlights of the other car flashed.

Bubba opened the door.

"Don't go, Bubba."

"You know, big brother," he said, "you ought to come with me. It would do you good to see how those ladies give me all that good X-rated sex they been holding out on their husbands all these years." He came around and opened my door. "Just stand outside and listen. She won't mind. Thrill to the days of yesteryear, big brother. Come along with me and I'll show you how good that low-rent lovin' can still be."

And, God help me, I did. My heart was pounding, but I stepped out of the car and followed my brother down the road in the moonlight.

"You know, Bubba, you are a devil. You have the damnedest way of getting people to do what you want."

"Don't I know it?"

"You were right about me being a gynecologist and all. Somehow, I lost interest in women. It just slipped away from me like everything else."

"The things closest to you go first," he said. "They slip away so softly you don't notice. You wake up one morning the stranger in a strange land."

"You're right," I said. "But women are . . . everything."

"Yea, verily, good buddy."

"Sex may be the secret of American life. In fact, I see now . . ."

But I don't know what I saw, for what happened next drove everything out of my head. The headlights of the car came on, blinding us, and we heard a male voice say, "Try to screw my wife, will you, you sons of bitches! I'll kill you!" Then a shotgun went off and I heard the shot rip through the air right over our heads. The car was rolling toward us and Bubba and I were running back down the road.

"The fence, big brother," Bubba shouted, "hit for the fence." And I dove under it, the barbed wire tearing the coat right off my back. Then we were stumbling through the prickly pear, the shotgun still going off and one pellet stinging the back of my neck like a yellow jacket.

Bubba grabbed me and threw me down. The car stopped and a spotlight probed around until it found us. Bubba leaped up, his fists balled, a foolhardy, magnificent sight. I thought: This is the end of your life, Ross.

Then we heard Floyd laughing and barking like a dog. "Come out, come out, wherever you are, Elvis."

It was all a big joke.

Bubba picked up a clod and threw it at the car, but Floyd only laughed harder. The band had been in on it—I could hear them laughing, too. My face was scratched and my palms were full of cactus thorns, and I could feel cold air on my back where my jacket had been ripped off.

Bubba climbed over the fence and threw himself at Floyd. They circled in the headlights, Bubba throwing wild punches and Floyd dodging them, shouting, "Shitfire and save matches, Bubba. Can't you take a joke?"

"Joke! We coulda been hurt running around in that god-damned cactus patch."

"Oh, hell, you're just pissed off 'cause we pulled that same trick on you in high school. I never thought you'd be stupid enough to fall for it twice."

That stopped Bubba. "All right," he said. "So I did. But this time it wasn't funny. We're grown men now, not high school kids."

Floyd kept laughing.

"All right, Floyd, you're fired. That's right. I'm giving you notice."

Somebody from the band stepped forward and said he thought Bubba was being too harsh, and Bubba fired him, too. He looked around and said, "Anybody else?"

Then everybody said it was fine with them; they were getting fed up with Bubba, anyway. There were some bitter words. It ended up with us going back to the motel and them going off to a honky-tonk to get drunk.

On the way back, Bubba began wondering where he was going to get another band. His troubles were multiplying and he said, "Maybe I should just shoot myself."

"Don't talk that way, Bubba."

At the motel, the television was still on, nothing showing on the screen now but snow. I went into the bathroom, threw my torn jacket in the trash can, and started putting iodine on the scratches on my face. The shot lifted me right off the floor.

He was sitting on the bed, holding the pistol. The television was exploded, a bullet through the picture tube. "I always wanted to know how he felt when he did that," Bubba said. "Now I know."

Things went downhill fast after that. My brother never found another band. The bookings dried up and Colonel Parker lost interest. The IRS was now investigating Bubba's income taxes, and in the middle of it all he got a Dear John letter from Nancy Jo saying she'd fallen in love with her psychiatrist.

He went down to Houston with the idea of confronting her but, instead, went to Calvin Sloate's house. Calvin himself answered the door and Bubba said, "I'm the son of a bitch who ran off with your wife."

"I know," Calvin said. "You're Bubba Moody. Come on in and let's let it all hang out."

Bubba, feeling numb all over, walked into Lisa's room. She was lying on her bed under a John Travolta poster.

"Your mother doesn't love me anymore," he said.

"I know. I think she's making a big mistake."

"You're the closest thing to her, the way she once was," Bubba said. "You're beautiful."

"Thanks, Bubba. I like your looks, too."

"Will you marry me?"

"Are you serious?"

"Dead serious," he said, and kissed her on her teenage lips.

When he turned around, Calvin was standing in the door.

Bubba phoned from Houston and said he'd been shot in the leg. It was nothing serious—Calvin had used a .22 target pistol. Before I left, I went over to tell Jan, who'd just gotten back from a trip to Las Vegas with Harley Otis. When I got there, she was gluing silver dollars to the top of the coffee table.

"Look here at all the money I won," she said. "Seems like my luck just won't quit."

When she heard about Bubba, she said, "That's his problem. All that's behind me now. I'm starting over."

She disappeared into the kitchen and I was left alone with the television. Tom Snyder was interviewing a judge in California who'd started divorcing fifty people in a group. There were no lawyers required, he just asked everyone if they had irreconcilable differences. When they said they did, he pronounced them divorced and they headed for the door. The men moved slowly, but the women were smiling and hopeful, and I thought how much better women seemed to adjust to modern life. "So would you say this is . . . the coming thing?" Tom Snyder asked, and the judge said it was.

"Notice anything different?" she said, coming back into the room.

"No. Is your hair shorter?"

She told me she'd had silicone injections. "Come on, Ross, you know my breasts always drooped."

"No, Jan. I've never noticed."

She put down her glass of white wine and lay on the floor. "See? They're nice and hard. They're the same standing up or laying down. They're just like doorknobs."

"I honestly can't tell the difference, Jan."

She leaned so close I could feel her breath on my cheek. "Go ahead and put your hand on them. I don't mind. Feel the difference for yourself."

I excused myself and drove home, the whole side of my face burning like I'd stood too close to a hot stove.

So Bubba never got his plastic surgery or a trip to Las Vegas (although his wife did). He ended up driving a truck again, but to me he seemed happier, and I found I enjoyed knowing him more than I had since we were kids. He still, however, had his problems with the IRS, and one night, in the dead of that winter, he tapped on my patio doors. We sat outside, in the darkness, while my wife watched *Family Feud*. (She seemed to draw strength from that program: She never missed it.)

121

"The government lawyers are coming Monday," Bubba said, "and I'm liable to do a couple of years in prison."

I told him I'd lend him money, but he said after the divorce he couldn't face going to court again.

"Let's take one last ride out Red River Road," he said, "in case I never see it again."

So we took a six-pack and drove out and parked on the edge of town, where the pumping jacks rose and fell in the fields on either side.

"You know," he said, "Elvis himself couldn't make it today. Everything today glorifies the loser, the person who can't help himself. Someone like me doesn't stand a chance. Yeah, it's the decade of the loser; and it's the losers who did me in. Come on, big brother, let's go ride those pumping jacks."

So we did. He could always talk me into anything. He sat on one end and I on the other, hanging on for dear life, and we rose and fell like two kids on a gigantic seesaw.

"Well, if that's the way this country's going to be," he shouted over the roar of the diesel, "they can have it. I want no part of it. I'll go right on, trying to do the impossible. Look, big brother," he said, reaching over his head as the pumping jack rose, "I can touch the moon."

Then he fell off. I thought he was dead. But he groaned and threw up in the weeds, and I cleaned him off as best I could.

"We'd better go home, Bubba," I said.

"He never died," Bubba said. "Not really."

"He did die, Bubba. Of a heart attack. We've all got to get older and die."

"No, big brother. I'll let you in on a secret. You and I are going to be the first people in history who don't."

The men from the IRS came on Monday, but Bubba was gone. Floyd, who was now back with the highway patrol, found his truck parked by the side of the road near Electra. There'd been lots of UFO sightings the night before. A farmer near Bowie found his cows dead, emptied out; nothing left of them but horns, hooves, and hide, and not a drop of blood on the ground, either. The lights of Bubba's truck were still on, and his CB radio, the key turned to SEND. Floyd found one footprint in the sandy soil just the other side of the fence, apparently headed for a strange depression in the ground, where all the grass was dead. It made the front page of the papers, and the sermon that Sunday was "A Close Encounter with Your God."

Then things got more or less back to normal here in Nortex. Bobby Joe Pitts started a marriage counseling service. He saw himself as someone who'd known the problem from both sides, a sort of Kissinger in the war between the sexes. Harley Otis got a divorce and married Jan, but it wasn't long before she showed up at Stolen Hours, a new bar for housewives where they could drink all afternoon, watch the soaps, and perhaps have a casual affair. Floyd forgot his grudge against Bubba and we spent several nights talking about all that had happened. "I'll tell you one thing," he said. "Your brother was the most remarkable person ever born around here."

In October, I finally made love to Nadine MacAfee. But we both discovered that what we had looked forward to for so long took only moments to do, and naturally this was a disappointment. We parted friends, but it confirmed my idea that the past is a closed book: You don't tamper with it.

But that night I couldn't sleep, and long after they played the national anthem on television, and showed the airplane and the prayer, I was still pacing the floor and feeling like a ghost. Then the phone rang.

"Hello, big brother."

For a moment I couldn't see or speak. "I just wanted to let you know," Bubba said, "I'm still on the planet Earth. In fact, I'm in Globe, Arizona."

"It's good to hear your voice, Bubba."

"It's good to hear yours. Hey, this is great country out here. Leaving that town was the best thing I ever did." He told me he was working as a disc jockey, but he had big plans. There was an old abandoned drive-in out on the edge of town, and he was going to renovate it and call it Bubba's Fifties Burger.

"You know," he said, "Carhops on roller skates, neon lights, and on the jukebox some of that great old rock and roll."

"Better keep a low profile, Bubba. You're still a wanted man."

"Don't worry about that," he said. "The road's right out my back door. And if I have to split, well, that won't be so bad either. If there's a prettier sight than an American blacktop road goin' nowhere in the moonlight, I don't know what it is."

There was a click, then nothing but echoes along one thousand miles of telephone cable.

Well, goddamn. I took three or four shots of Jack Daniel's and did a sort of dance out there on my patio, hopping around under the stars. Then I got in the car to go tell Floyd the good news: that the King was still with us.

SHELBY HEARON

The Undertow of Friends

My friends and I can talk for hours, we women who came of age together. We are attentive to the same details, each caring to the same extent. We don't tire of one another's lives. We cover everyone: mothers, sons, lovers, in-laws. No one who is not us cares about these people in the same proportion or to the same degree. Some, who love a particular family member, care for that one; while others, friends or former spouses, care for none.

George has his own friends too; they go back to the start, and I am no part of them. I can hear their stories but I cannot weigh them fairly. Some strike me as too odd, too pointless, some too harsh to be treated in a joking way.

I often worry that we, Jean and George, a recent couple without a past in common, will never keep afloat. You read about custody fights and ex-spouses as a strain on a relationship, but no one talks about the undertow of friends.

*　　*　　*

When I was small, I lived in the little town of Katy, Texas, named for the railroad that runs like a river from the piney woods to the coast.

Every afternoon I would cross two dirt side streets, scramble up a clay bank, and walk under a stand of dark pines to my best friend's house to play with her brother's dog. I was allowed to go alone because in small towns young girls could go where they liked, under the unspoken watch of neighbors.

Most afternoons she, Sally, would come back home with me because she liked to eat at our house and because my daddy would stop what he was doing and give her some little treat to take home: a cornshuck doll, a tiny rabbit carved from soap, an armload of heavy amethyst hydrangeas.

I was jealous of her until I got the message that my daddy was doing it because he knew her folks and that Sally only hung around my daddy because she didn't have one of her own who was any account.

Grown, both living in the state capital, we still call each other often and see each other when we can, when I'm not busy with my classes and Sally's not weighed down with the strain of being cheery about her ten-year affair with a married legislator and the burden of two aging Labrador retrievers.

George does not understand my attachment to her and arranges to be gone when she comes by.

He grew up in West Texas, and his pals are the good old boys who amble from side to side when they walk, as if they just dismounted from a horse.

His best friend, Archer, went through undergraduate days with him, got his final degree with him at Rice, also suffered the end of a painful early marriage, and has been a colleague of his in the math department at Texas for a dozen years.

George thinks Archer is a sketch and never tires of his friend's imitations of himself: " 'This is your life, Archer Clovis.' . . . 'Why, hello, Dad, I haven't seen you since you stole the sheriff's car and sold it back to him.'" He and Archer have a routine in which they found Clovis University, the Harvard of the Southwest, the pearl in the oyster of the Gulf, staffed only by themselves. And George delights in all its variations.

This year Archer has been on sabbatical in Madison, Wisconsin, also a capital–university town laid out on a river. George gave him a farewell dinner complete with a horseshoe of real red roses and a speech that ended: "Henceforth you will go into the world and pass for normal. Strangers will mistake you for a mechanical engineer. Nubile graduate students will offer themselves."

Archer calls George every week, or George calls him. He sent us a frozen squirrel, fourth-class mail, in a package marked RABID: HANDLE WITH CARE. In return, George invented a fat Swedish girlfriend for Archer, who has none, to keep him warm against the cold, and sent them both long underwear.

Crowded by these antics from the past in our rented blue-walled rooms, I tell George, "We need a place of our own."

"What's wrong with this house?"

"I mean a place which knows us only in the present, Jean and George."

After the third time that Sally calls while we are making love beneath the dainty underbellies of the doves who peck at our skylight, George agrees. The next day he announces, "I found us a café."

It is called the Library Annex, and we make ourselves at home at once, going there almost every afternoon at the end of classes to have a pint of sun-brewed tea and a roasted-pork sandwich with homemade mayonnaise and banana peppers on hot fresh bread. We sit on the same side of the back corner booth, close together, enjoying the ambience and speaking only to strangers.

The place gets its name from the fact that the owner (a man named Howie, who wears a workshirt and apron and ties his hair back with a rubber band) wanted to open a bookstore but was afraid of failure, and so instead opened a restaurant next to a branch library, imagining a horde of thirsty readers with their arms full of thick summertime novels wanting a place to sit and wipe their buttery fingers and turn their enthralling pages.

It is a lovely space with booths along the wall, big wooden children's tables in the center, blue willow crockery, and blue-and-white-striped awnings on the inside. When the awnings are at half-mast against the glaring sun, the light draws a line on the blue-and-white vinyl floor, making the room seem at once open and closed. Voices carry; the slightest gesture on the part of anyone causes you to look up and smile. It is both a public and a private place, off the beaten path in a residential area, and we promise that we will share it with no one.

Then Archer calls to say he is to have his back operated on. He has been in pain for weeks, he relates. Then on his way to class today his left foot refused to function. "It flopped like a fish. Just imagine," he tells George, "in the old days you had to live with it. Dragged around like a lame dog. The doctor says they used to call it lumbago and send you home. Now he says I'll be back on the courts in two weeks, never mind that I haven't played in years." George relays that his friend's voice has grown edgy and brittle, even when he tries to joke.

"He ought to have somebody with him," he tells me. "I should go up."

"Maybe he'd rather you waited until he felt good again?"

"No, when you want someone is when things are bad."

George broods. He tells me again about the time Archer, at age nine, won the state Soap Box Derby and got a medal before a crowd of seventy-five thousand in Memorial Stadium—and his family missed it all, lost in the east parking lot. About how Archer's sons from his early marriage have a new daddy who possesses a Cessna, a Porsche, and ski-slope expertise.

"He shouldn't be alone." Fretting, he bundles off a cut-

and-paste booklet replete with bosoms and legs, for reading in Clovis General.

That afternoon we linger longer than usual in the Annex, appreciating the shift of scene in the air when people enter: the way voices die down, gestures stop, eyes blink, and then—reassured that we are all safe in the lovely blue-and-white room with its slanted light—the commotion begins again.

Today while we are preparing classes (which for me means returning to the richness of the Middle Ages that seem such a marvel coming from tiny, uneventful Katy, Texas), Archer calls to say the deed is done.

"How do you feel?" George asks.

"Euphoric," Archer swears, although George reports that his voice has a new breakable quality even as he does an imitation of his old self. "The nurses mistake me for a mechanical engineer. The one named Olga is teaching me to say, 'Take off your clothes,' in Swedish. One week from today I'll be playing at Wimbledon. 'This is your life, Archer Clovis, medical miracle.'"

"I ought to come up," George says.

"No way. My old man is here. He's decided to help me sue the university and the shuttle-bus company and the last girl I was with."

George is hurt. Off the phone he opens a Lone Star. He is depressed by the idea that Archer would invent a family to keep him from coming up. "His old man's been dead for ten years at least," he tells me.

"Do you want to see a movie later?"

"We'll see." He gathers his things together. "Maybe I should go anyway?"

"He has his pride."

As we get ready to leave, George decides he isn't up to the Annex this afternoon, that we will go tomorrow, that he may work in his office until suppertime.

"I'll see what Sally is up to," I tell him.

129

*   *   *

When I meet her by the fountain, she looks the same—bright red turtleneck, sunglasses and lipstick matching, boots, her mane of hair flying—but I can see the cracks in her the way you can see the veins in an old person's temple.

"He changed his mind about renting us an apartment," she says into the bustle of forty thousand students going by. "Said it was too risky, at least for now, when he has reelection to think about."

I grab her arm and tell her to come with me, that I have someplace special to show her, guaranteed to cheer her up.

As we walk to the Annex, she tells me that her old hounds are getting too feeble to keep, incontinent, forgetful; that she's thinking of letting them go to her brother's ranch.

We walk in the door, breaking the sunlight, and sit at a table in the center, which I have never done before. As we order our Mason jars of iced tea and the roasted pork on home-made bread, I look up and see George—having a beer in our usual booth, listening to a story that Howie, in his workshirt and apron, is relating.

"So we come home, see, and we've been up at the lake, and we're water-logged and baked out, and the phone is ringing. I pick it up, and this strange man demands, 'Where is my daughter?'

"'Who is your daughter?' I ask him. It turns out that my son Mike met her at a party and went off with her, and she never came home. Her parents were ready to call the police when Mike phoned her father and said: 'I'm out on my dad's boat, sir, and the cotter pin is out. We're stranded on Lake Travis, but he's bringing one to me.'"

"Beautiful," George says, laughing. "Truly. You don't even own a boat, right?"

"Never have. But that's not the clincher." Howie leans down. "I say, 'Let me get back to you, sir, after I contact my son on the ship-to-shore radio.'"

"Perfect." George lifts his mug.

"So then I drive over to Mike's room and bang on the door and I tell them about the father's call, and they break up laughing. She is in this shirt of his, there are about two dozen longnecks on the shag rug. They haven't been outside for twenty-four hours." Howie delivers the kill: "Get this, George. I look at her and say, 'If you don't mind my asking, honey, how old are you?'"

"And?"

"Twenty-five. Twenty-five and not home all night." Howie heads for the kitchen, slapping his forehead.

I raise my tea glass slightly, and George meets my eyes.

I don't get Howie's tale at all. Do not understand why it is funny that his son lied to the girl's father, or why it is amusing that the father wanted to know where his daughter was, even at twenty-five. I am a woman, and, cut by Archer's life (What if we don't need each other the way we thought?), George has gone back to the safety of men.

I concentrate on getting the appearance of the room exactly, the knives and forks, the smell of hot bread, the blue willow plates, the chilled tea glasses with their wedges of lemon, the motion of crumbs brushed from the smooth polished tabletops. The filtered afternoon grade-school light which draws its line across the waxed Annex floor: girls on one side, boys on the other.

George nods his head toward Sally, and I nod back, acknowledging that in our hour of need, we all return to where we came from.

My best friend, unaware of what is past her shoulder, has brightened up over the unexpected treat of the new place. She takes a giant bite of her sandwich and, fortified, decides that she will get a new pair of puppies, playful young dogs. That maybe she will even tell the legislator to go back to his wife when the session is over. "Do you think your daddy would take me back?" she asks, laughing at our old joke.

★
LARRY L. KING

Something Went with Daddy

R ight after supper Mama
started acting all fidgety,
picking at the dingy old doily on her armchair like she was
working a blackberry patch and staring at nothing with her
blank, Orphan-Annie eyes while she hummed little snatches of
songs. Church songs, mostly, though now and again I recognized notes of "Buffalo Gals" and "Old Joe Clark" and "Sally
Goodin." Songs from a happier time, when her and Daddy
used to square dance half the night at socials along the creek-
banks, though Lord knows that's been so long dirt and water
must of been young.

When Mama gets fidgety I always start feeling shaky. I
know within reason what she's working up to talk about. And
I also know that my wife, Merlie, won't never let it pass without a yow-yow.

Sure enough. Mama said, "That first night I seen Jesus, I

didn't have no notion it was him. Thought it was just one of them silly ol' hippies wrapped up in a bedsheet that had broke in the house someway. Until I seen his eyes. Then I said to myself, 'Mabellene, there ain't no hippie on this good earth got eyes like that.' Nawsir. They was like green coals of fire, them eyes. They give it away he was Jesus, don't you see? That, and him walking flat-dab through my bedroom wall purty as you please."

Merlie, being small-minded about Mama's visits from Jesus, shot me a disgusted look and jumped up from the couch to turn TV on. She flicked the knob all around but couldn't find any game shows, just a wrestling match from Houston and a bunch of news programs. Merlie thinks wrestling's tacky and news a waste of time, so I was hoping she'd light on a game show.

I heard little bits about a car wreck, a fire blamed on kids playing with matches and a sawyer over close to Lufkin shooting his brother-in-law when they fell out over a poker game. Shot him dead quicker than it takes to tell it, over thirty-some dollars. More than likely bad blood from way back was at the bottom of it. TV don't always tell things right. When Daddy was fresh disappeared they made a botch of half they told.

Merlie breathed like she'd run a steep hill, the way she does when she's worked up, and kept spinning the dial past the same programs over and over. Mama's fingers kept snicking at the doily and she said, "Sure as I set here it was sweet Jesus hisself. Tell me you ever seen a ol' hippie walk through somebody's wall and not even leave a hole."

"Nome," I said.

"I guess Merlie thinks *she* has," Mama said, like Merline wadn't even in the room. Merlie give a snort and turned off TV with a loud click that sounded like somebody cocking a pistol.

"Now, Mama," I said. "Be nice, Mama."

"Try telling *her* to be nice," Mama said.

"Tell *her* I hadn't said a blessed word," Merlie said. "Tell her I'm just minding my own bidness and wish others could say the same."

I dearly despise it when they put me in the middle. Lately it's happening more and more, which makes me so shaky I don't sleep good for nights on end.

"I can tell Missy Merlie don't believe I've laid eyes on Jesus a single time in my whole life," Mama said. "Never mind nine nights a-running."

"Tell your mama I am a *married* woman, not a 'Missy,'" Merlie snapped, "and tell her my eyes can't believe in what they ain't *seen!*"

"Tell her she ain't likely to see Jesus at some old roadside honky-tonk," Mama said. "I know for a fact Jesus don't drink beer."

"Cleetus, your mama knows good and well it wadn't no honky-tonk to it," Merlie said. "It was a truck stop cafe, and I didn't work there but three months. And *that* was on account of you being out of work that last time. *Somebody's* got to put meat on the table around here!"

Merlie jumped up from the couch and sashayed to the kitchen with her nose in the air. Anytime Merlie and Mama gets into it, she goes in and fixes herself a snack or sometimes a whole big meal with gravy and pie. Merlie's put on weight like a growing shoat since Mama come to live with us nearly three years ago after something went with Daddy.

Mama didn't take notice of Merlie leaving. She said, "Jesus don't even drink wine like some people claims."

"Yessum," I said.

"Preacher Gaskins says Jesus turned water into *grape juice* not *wine,* way back yonder. Says it was clear as you please in the Bible until some silly professor copied down the Scriptures wrong and fooled the faithless. Probably on a-purpose."

Mama's fingers picked and flew at the doily faster and faster. I had to bite my tongue to keep from yelling for her to stop her dang fidgeting. She looked up with her old hands still working and said, "Cleetus, I never will be able to reckon why you married that girl."

I've tried to reckon the same thing many a time myself, but never out loud. So I just said, "Be nice, Mama. Please."

"It ain't gonna last," Mama said. And set her face like a bunched fist.

"Now, Mama," I said. "It's already lasted close on to seven years."

"And what you got to show for it?" Mama shot back. "Not even a sweet little baby I could rock and sing to and tell all about me and Jesus. Ought to be *one* person around this place to care about that. I'd call up that paper again if I thought it'd do a nickel's worth of good."

"No, Mama," I said, real quick. "You know how worked up Merlie got the time that reporter come out here to the house."

"All in the world that paper boy done was ask smart-aleck questions trying to make a fool out of me," Mama said. "He never wrote down a blessed word I said. I don't know why in the Sam Hill he bothered coming out here."

I knew why. See, Mama'd phoned the dang newspaper and said Jesus had give her a bunch of Bible Scriptures to look up and told her if she could puzzle 'em out right then she'd know what had went with Daddy. The reporter who come out to the house asked reckon why Jesus hadn't told her flat out, if he'd truly wanted her to know. "It was like a riddle Jesus give me," Mama had told him. "Sort of a test. Bible says the Lord moves in mysterious ways, you know."

The whole thing had made Merlie fit to be tied. She said if anything come out in the paper about Mama and a green-eyed Jesus playing detective together, she'd go down to the court-house and sign papers to have Mama put away. Which led to about the biggest fuss me and Merlie ever had.

"If you ask me," Mama said, "we got the sorriest excuse for a paper in East Texas. Can't any old pus-gutted politician or cowboy singer come within a hunnert miles of Lanville without they splash stories and pictures all across the front page. But just you try and get 'em to put *Jesus'* name in the paper when he's here."

I heard the eggbeater whining and whirring in the kitchen and said, "Mama, now, you're just gonna have to hush your gabbling about that stuff. You've went and made Merlie bake a cake or a pie, and you know she don't need it with high blood pressure."

Mama said, "Cleetus Boatright, if anybody'd told me I'd live to see my own boy say I can't call the sweet precious name of Jesus in my own house . . ." She put her head down and commenced sniffling.

"*Whose* house did she say?" Merlie yelled from the kitchen. "You tell her this was *my* house and my daddy's house before I knew either one of y'all. And it'll be my house till I *die*!"

Mama raised her voice and said, "Tell Missy Merlie I don't talk to honky-tonk girls, I don't care *how* many houses they claim to own."

"Be *nice,* Mama," I said. "You want maybe to look at that new Sears & Roebuck wish book awhile? You can take a pencil and make your Christmas list."

"What good would it do?" Mama said. "You know how Merlie grudges ever nickel I cost. She'd let me starve if she thought she might get away with it."

"Shush, Mama!" I said. "Don't talk so dang loud!"

But I'd spoke too late. There stood Merlie in the door, her eyes spitting fire. She said, "Tell your mama I believe that's the meanest thing I ever heard a white woman say!"

"Cleetus, son," Mama whined, "it wadn't half as mean as the meanness she says to me when you ain't here. That girl talks to me like I'm some mangy old yard dog."

"Tell her *no wonder* your daddy up and run off," Merlie yelled, her face going all red and splotchy. "He couldn't stand living with a storytelling old crazy woman another cockeyed minute!"

Mama said, "Now *that's* the meanest thing *I* ever heard a white woman say!" She commenced crying big and wrapped her face in her hands. Merlie started clamoring awful hurting talk about Mama being a pest and a body tick, as loud and fast as a tobacco auctioneer.

"Be *nice!*" I yelled. "*Both of you!* God *dang* it!"

My shaky feeling was getting so bad it was making me dizzy. They both hushed, looking a little bit scared. I softened down my voice and put a grin on and said, "Lordee mercy me, y'all *both* know I got to work tomorrow! Jobs don't grow on trees around here!" I figured that to quieten 'em down, and it did. I'd lost jobs at the sawmill, the lumberyard and reading gas meters for the city over in Orange when my shakiness had got so bad I couldn't work. When my shakiness reaches a certain point about all I'm good for is fishing, off by myself and as far away from the world as I can manage.

Merlie turned and padded on back to the kitchen, her house shoes making them doubled-under flippety-flop noises I don't like because somehow it sounds to me like a crippled horse trying to run. I dried Mama's tears on my shirttail and seen the hair was thinner than winter grass on her bowed old white head. She grabbed my hand, kissing it and nuzzling it up against her wet old face. I stood real still, feeling hot and clumsy, not ever being partial to close touching. I don't think I even liked it as a baby.

Mama said, "Oh, hunny, things wouldn't be near so bad if something hadn't went with your daddy."

"I know it, Mama," I said. "But we can't change that."

She commenced fresh crying. I give her one of my red bandanas that I have to wear working at Kiddieland West, where I lead Shetland ponies around in a big circle while noisy kids play like they're cowboys and cowgirls. Sometimes the real little ones bawl their lungs out, scratching and kicking me when I try to gentle them down. It can make a long day.

Mama honked her nose in the bandana and said, "Cleetus, hunny, can I have my Bible?"

"Not now, Mama," I said. "You'd just look up them certain Scriptures and puzzle about Daddy half the dang night. We all need our rest."

She just stared off at nothing, looking shrunk, while her bony old fingers flew over the chair doily in little nips and tucks as fast as she'd picked cotton when I was a kid. I couldn't abide anymore of those snick-snack sounds, and went to the kitchen hoping for fresh coffee.

Merlie looked up from eating cold fried salmon cakes and deviled eggs while waiting for her sweets to cook, her jaws bulging like a squirrel storing up winter nuts. I went to the stove and turned on the gas under that morning's coffee. I miss wood-burning stoves. There's a lot I miss from way back. Peace and quiet, for one thing.

Merlie said, "Cleetus, you ought not drink coffee this late. Much trouble as you have sleeping." That woman gives so much dang advice I wonder why she didn't make a lawyer, but I didn't say a mumbling word. Just turned to watch her eat, against my judgment. Eating ought to be fun but Merlie, I dunno, she goes at it like it's a job of work. Still and all, I can't help but watch when she's stuffing herself. It's like I'm under a dark spell.

Between bites Merlie mumbled, "I sure hope your mama's simmering down."

"Maybe she'll doze off directly," I said.

Merlie heaved a fat sigh and said, "I bet we won't much more'n get stretched out in bed good until she starts talking out loud to her green-eyed Jesus."

I took a deep breath and said, "Merlie, now, if she does then I don't want you going to her room to fuss at her. Mama says ever time you do, Jesus ups and leaves." Merlie snorted, rolled her eyes, and stuffed in another wad of salmon cake. "I don't see it hurts for Mama to talk to Jesus," I said. "He's all the poor old soul's got since something went with Daddy."

I turned to slosh coffee in my cup. Behind me, I could hear Merlie cleaning her fingers with awful sucking sounds. One swallow of that warmed-over, bitter old black boiled coffee persuaded me I didn't want more. I didn't know for sure what I wanted. Not feeling so shaky would of been a good start. Being able to turn life back and start over, maybe, to before I'd got hooked up with so many folks that seemed to like fussing and wrangling all the time. My mind surprised me by suddenly thinking how much it missed my school days, until I studied it over and decided what I really missed was playing hookey to go fishing or hunting and the sense of being free it'd always give me. But life's harder to play hookey from than school, and you can't turn it back like you can an alarm clock. I went to the sink intending to pour out my coffee.

Merlie finished sucking her fingers clean and said, "Cleetus, now don't get mad, I know he was your daddy and all. But try to recollect how shaky he made *you* them last few years. All that heavy drinking. Yelling his head off if somebody crossed him, pounding his walking cane on the floor if his meals was two minutes late, making your mama cry for no reason except meanness that I could see." She paused and then said with a shiver in her voice, "And that time he . . . put his hands on me."

"No need to count all that up again, Merlie," I said, hearing it come out kind of strangled.

"Cleetus, I'm just reminding you that when your mama cries and carries on about him you shouldn't get so upset. She'd got to where *she* could hardly stand him until—"

"Hush, dang it!" I hollered and whirled back to face her. Merlie half jumped up from the kitchen table, like she might bolt to run, until she seen me make myself relax and lean against the counter. I never have hit Merlie, don't get the wrong idea. Come close a few times, maybe, but close don't count except in horseshoes.

I felt a stinging in my hand, then something wet, and looked down to see I'd squeezed a crack in my coffee cup. Coffee was mixing with blood. I turned around to wash my hand and the cracked cup in the sink, hoping Merlie hadn't noticed. The sludgy coffee leavings, mixed with blood, reminded me of some swamp scene I maybe remembered from a scary old movie but I pushed it from my head.

In a minute Merlie said in her kindly voice, like she might be soothing a spooked horse, "Cleetus, sweetie, now you know you don't want to miss work tomorrow." I nodded, wiped the last trickle of blood on my britches and turned to see her eating again. Little bits of salmon cake and deviled eggs sprayed from her mouth onto the oilcloth showing The Lord's Supper, which I'd bought for Mama last Christmas, making it look like Jesus and the disciples had pink and yellow freckles.

I looked away and said in a real soft voice, "Merlie, let's *all* try to be nice. Me. You. Mama. The world don't have near enough of nice."

Merlie blinked and said, "Cleetus, maybe you better sleep in the wash house tonight." I give her a quick look. I hate sleeping in that dang old wash house on that old couch with the broke-down springs and the smell of detergents and wet wash. On the other hand, it's not much of a treat anymore to sleep with Merlie. So I just nodded. Merlie said mighty quick, "Not that I wouldn't be proud to have you. It's just that when you get all shaky and toss and turn all night . . ."

"Don't fret over it," I said. "Nighty-night, Merlie." She set back and started to relax before saying, "Oh, my *pie!*" and jumping up to run for a potholder.

I walked out in the back yard and stood still under a tall pine tree for the longest time, feeling near about as shaky as I ever had, seeing a night sky full of stars where nobody could ever bother me if I could just somehow get to one. Thinking: *I got to take one of 'em fishing back in Big Thicket Creek soon.* I hadn't made up my mind which one to ask, but I figured it wouldn't make much difference. Can't either one of 'em swim a dang stroke. Daddy, he couldn't swim neither.

REGINALD McKNIGHT

The Kind of Light That Shines on Texas

I never liked Marvin Pruitt. Never liked him, never knew him, even though there were only three of us in the class. Three black kids. In our school there were fourteen classrooms of thirty-odd white kids (in '66, they considered Chicanos provisionally white) and three or four black kids. Primary school in primary colors. Neat division. Alphabetized. They didn't stick us in the back, or arrange us by degrees of hue, apartheidlike. This was real integration, a ten-to-one ratio as tidy as upper-class landscaping. If it all worked, you could have ten white kids all to yourself. They could talk to you, get the feel of you, scrutinize you bone deep if they wanted to. They seldom wanted to, and that was fine with me for two reasons. The first was that their scrutiny was irritating. How do you comb your hair—why do you comb your hair—may I please touch your hair—were the kinds of questions they asked. This is no way to feel at home. The second reason was Marvin. He embarrassed me. He smelled bad, was at least two grades behind, was hostile, dark skinned, homely, close-mouthed. I feared him for his size, pitied him for his dress, watched him all the time. Marveled at him, mystified, astonished, uneasy.

He had the habit of spitting on his right arm, juicing it down till it would glisten. He would start in immediately after taking his seat when we'd finished with the Pledge of Allegiance, "The Yellow Rose of Texas," "The Eyes of Texas Are upon You," and "Mistress Shady." Marvin would rub his spit-flecked arm with his left hand, rub and roll as if polishing an ebony pool cue. Then he would rest his head in the crook of his arm, sniffing, huffing deep like black-jacket boys huff bagsful of acrylics. After ten minutes or so, his eyes would close, heavy. He would sleep till recess. Mrs. Wickham would let him.

There was one other black kid in our class. A girl they called Ah-so. I never learned what she did to earn this name. There was nothing Asian about this big-shouldered girl. She was the tallest, heaviest kid in school. She was quiet, but I don't think any one of us was subtle or sophisticated enough to nickname our classmates according to any but physical attributes. Fat kids were called Porky or Butterball, skinny ones were called Stick or Ichabod. Ah-so was big, thick, and African. She would impassively sit, sullen, silent as Marvin. She wore the same dark blue pleated skirt every day, the same ruffled white blouse every day. Her skin always shone as if worked by Marvin's palms and fingers. I never spoke one word to her, nor she to me.

Of the three of us, Mrs. Wickham called only on Ah-so and me. Ah-so never answered one question, correctly or incorrectly, so far as I can recall. She wasn't stupid. When asked to read aloud she read well, seldom stumbling over long words, reading with humor and expression. But when Wickham asked her about Farmer Brown and how many cows, or the capital of Vermont, or the date of this war or that, Ah-so never spoke. Not one word. But you always felt she could have answered those questions if she'd wanted to. I sensed no tension, embarrassment, or anger in Ah-so's reticence. She simply refused to speak. There was something unshakable about her, some core so impenetrably solid, you got the feeling that if you stood too close to her she could eat your thoughts like a black star eats light. I didn't despise Ah-so as I despised Marvin. There was nothing malevolent about her. She sat like a great icon in the back of the classroom, tranquil, guarded, sealed up, watchful. She was close to sixteen, and it was my guess she'd given up on school. Perhaps she was just obliging the wishes of her family, sticking it out till the law could no longer reach her.

There were at least half a dozen older kids in our class. Besides Marvin and Ah-so there was Oakley, who sat behind me, whispering threats into my ear; Varna Willard with the large breasts; Eddie Limon, who played bass for a high school rock band; and Lawrence Ridderbeck, who everyone said had a kid and a wife. You couldn't expect me to know anything about Texan educational practices of the 1960s, so I never knew why there were so many older kids in my sixth-grade class. After all, I was just a boy and had transferred into the school around midyear. My father, an air force sergeant, had been sent to Viet Nam. The air force sent my mother, my sister, Claire, and me to Connolly Air Force Base, which during the war housed "unaccompanied wives." I'd been to so many different schools in my short life that I ceased wondering about their differences. All I knew about the Texas schools is that they weren't afraid to flunk you.

Yet though I was only twelve then, I had a good idea why Wickham never once called on Marvin, why she let him snooze in the crook of his polished arm. I knew why she would press her lips together, and narrow her eyes at me whenever I correctly answered a question, rare as that was. I know why she badgered Ah-so with questions everyone knew Ah-so would never even consider answering. Wickham didn't like us. She wasn't gross about it, but it was clear she didn't want us around. She would prove her dislike day after day with little stories and jokes. "I just want to share with you all," she would say, "a little riddle my daughter told me at the supper table th'other day. Now, where do you go when you injure your knee?" Then one, two, or all three of her pets would say for the rest of us, "We don't know, Miz Wickham," in that skin-chilling way suck-asses speak, "where?" "Why, to Africa," Wickham would say, "where the knee grows."

The thirty-odd white kids would laugh, and I would look across the room at Marvin. He'd be asleep. I would glance back at Ah-so. She'd be sitting still as a projected image, staring down at her desk. I, myself, would smile at Wickham's stupid jokes, sometimes fake a laugh. I tried to show her that at least one of us was alive and alert, even though her jokes hurt. I sucked ass, too, I suppose. But I wanted her to understand more than anything that I was not like her other nigra children, that I was worthy of more than the non-attention and the neg-ative attention she paid Marvin and Ah-so. I hated her, but never showed it. No one could safely contradict that woman. She knew all kinds of tricks to demean, control, and punish you. And she could swing her two-foot paddle as fluidly as a big-league slugger swings a bat. You didn't speak in Wickham's class unless she spoke to you first. You didn't chew gum, or wear "hood" hair. You didn't drag your feet, curse, pass notes, hold hands with the opposite sex. Most especially, you didn't say anything bad about the Aggies, Governor Connolly, LBJ, Sam Houston, or Waco. You did the forbidden and she would get you. It was that simple.

She never got me, though. Never gave her reason to. But she could have invented reasons. She did a lot of that. I can't be sure, but I used to think she pitied me because my father was in Viet Nam and my uncle A. J. had recently died there. When-ever she would tell one of her racist jokes, she would always glance at me, preface the joke with, "Now don't you nigra children take offense. This is all in fun, you know. I just want to share with you all something Coach Gilchrest told me th'other day." She would tell her joke, and glance at me again. I'd giggle, feeling a little queasy. "I'm half Irish," she would chuckle, "and you should hear some of those Irish jokes." She never told any, and I never really expected her to. I just did my Tom-thing. I kept my shoes shined, my desk neat, answered her questions as best I could, never brought gum to school, never cursed, never slept in class. I wanted to show her we were not all the same.

I tried to show them all, all thirty-odd, that I was different. It worked to some degree, but not very well. When some article was stolen from someone's locker or desk, Marvin, not I, was the first accused. I'd be second. Neither Marvin, nor Ah-so nor I were ever chosen for certain classroom honors—"Pledge leader," "flag holder," "noise monitor," "paper passer outer," but Mrs. Wickham once let me be "eraser duster." I was proud. I didn't even care about the cracks my fellow students made about my finally having turned the right color. I had done something that Marvin, in the deeps of his never-ending sleep, couldn't even dream of doing. Jack Preston, a kid who sat in front of me, asked me one day at recess whether I was embarrassed about Marvin. "Can you believe that guy?" I said. "He's like a pig or something. Makes me sick."

"Does it make you ashamed to be colored?"

"No," I said, but I meant yes. Yes, if you insist on thinking us all the same. Yes, if his faults are mine, his weaknesses inherent in me.

"I'd be," said Jack.

I made no reply. I was ashamed. Ashamed for not defending Marvin and ashamed that Marvin even existed. But if it had occurred to me, I would have asked Jack whether he was ashamed of being white because of Oakley. Oakley, "Oak Tree," Kelvin "Oak Tree" Oakley. He was sixteen and proud of it. He made it clear to everyone, including Wickham, that his life's ambition was to stay in school one more year, till he'd be old enough to enlist in the army. "Them slopes got my brother," he would say. "I'mna sign up and git me a few slopes. Gonna kill them bastards deader'n shit." Oakley, so far as anyone knew, was and always had been the oldest kid in his family. But no one contradicted him. He would, as anyone would tell you, "snap yer neck jest as soon as look at you." Not a boy in class, excepting Marvin and myself, had been able to avoid Oakley's pink bellies, Texas titty twisters, moon pie punches, or worse. He didn't bother Marvin, I suppose, because Marvin was closer to his size and age, and because Marvin spent five sixths of the school day asleep. Marvin probably never crossed Oakley's mind. And to say that Oakley hadn't bothered me is not to say he had no intention of ever doing so. In fact, this haphazard sketch of hairy fingers, slash of eyebrow, explosion of acne, elbows, and crooked teeth, swore almost daily that he'd like to kill me.

Naturally, I feared him. Though we were about the same height, he outweighed me by no less than forty pounds. He talked, stood, smoked, and swore like a man. No one, except for Mrs. Wickham, the principal, and the coach, ever laid a finger on him. And even Wickham knew that the hot lines she laid on him merely amused him. He would smile out at the classroom, goofy and bashful, as she laid down the two, five, or maximum ten strokes on him. Often he would wink, or surreptitiously flash us the thumb as Wickham worked on him. When she was finished, Oakley would walk so cool back to his seat you'd think he was on wheels. He'd slide into his chair, sniff the air, and say, "Somethin's burnin. Do y'all smell smoke? I swanee, I smell smoke and fahr back here." If he had made these cracks and never threatened me, I might have grown to admire Oakley, even liked him a little. But he hated me, and took every opportunity during the six-hour school day to make me aware of this. "Some Sambo's gittin his ass broke open one of these days," he'd mumble. "I wanna fight somebody. Need to keep in shape till I git to Nam."

I never said anything to him for the longest time. I pretended not to hear him, pretended not to notice his sour breath on my neck and ear. "Yep," he'd whisper. "Coonies keep y' in good shape for slope killin." Day in, day out, that's the kind of thing I'd pretend not to hear. But one day when the rain dropped down like lead balls, and the cold air made your skin look plucked, Oakley whispered to me, "My brother tells me it rains like this in Nam. Maybe I oughta go out at recess and break your ass open today. Nice and cool so you don't sweat. Nice and wet to clean up the blood." I said nothing for at least half a minute, then I turned half right and said, "Thought you said your brother was dead." Oakley, silent himself, for a time, poked me in the back with his pencil and hissed, "*Yer* dead." Wickham cut her eyes our way, and it was over.

It was hardest avoiding him in gym class. Especially when we played murderball. Oakley always aimed his throws at me. He threw with unblinking intensity, his teeth gritting, his neck veining, his face flushing, his black hair sweeping over one eye. He could throw hard, but the balls were squishy and harmless. In fact, I found his misses more intimidating than his hits. The balls would whiz by, thunder against the folded bleachers. They rattled as though a locomotive were passing through them. I would duck, dodge, leap as if he were throwing grenades. But he always hit me, sooner or later. And after a while I noticed that the other boys would avoid throwing at me, as if I belonged to Oakley.

One day, however, I was surprised to see that Oakley was throwing at everyone else but me. He was uncommonly accurate, too; kids were falling like tin cans. Since no one was throwing at me, I spent most of the game watching Oakley cut this one and that one down. Finally, he and I were the only ones left on the court. Try as he would, he couldn't hit me, nor I him. Coach Gilchrest blew his whistle and told Oakley and me to bring the red rubber balls to the equipment locker. I was relieved I'd escaped Oakley's stinging throws for once. I was feeling triumphant, full of myself. As Oakley and I approached Gilchrest, I thought about saying something friendly to Oakley: Good game, Oak Tree, I would say. Before I could speak, though, Gilchrest said, "All right boys, there's five minutes left in the period. Y'all are so good, looks like, you're gonna have to play like men. No boundaries, no catch outs, and you gotta hit your opponent three times in order to win. Got me?"

We nodded.

"And you're gonna use these," said Gilchrest, pointing to three volleyballs at his feet. "And you better believe they're pumped full. Oates, you start at that end of the court. Oak Tree, you're at th'other end. Just like usual, I'll set the balls at mid-court, and when I blow my whistle I want y'all to haul your cheeks to the middle and th'ow for all you're worth. Got me?" Gilchrest nodded at our nods, then added, "Remember, no boundaries, right?"

I at my end, Oakley at his, Gilchrest blew his whistle. I was faster than Oakley and scooped up a ball before he'd covered three quarters of his side. I aimed, threw, and popped him right on the knee. "One–zip!" I heard Gilchrest shout. The ball bounced off his knee and shot right back into my hands. I hurried my throw and missed. Oakley bent down, clutched the two remaining balls. I remember being amazed that he could palm each ball, run full out, and throw left-handed or right-handed without a shade of awkwardness. I spun, ran, but one of Oakley's throws glanced off the back of my head. "One–one!" hollered Gilchrest. I fell and spun on my ass as the other ball came sailing at me. I caught it. "He's out!" I yelled. Gilchrest's voice boomed, "No catch outs. Three hits. Three hits." I leapt to my feet as Oakley scrambled across the floor for another ball. I chased him down, leapt, and heaved the ball hard as he drew himself erect. The ball hit him dead in the face, and he went down flat. He rolled around, cupping his hands over his nose. Gilchrest sped to his side, helped him to his feet, asked him whether he was OK. Blood flowed from Oakley's nose, dripped in startlingly bright spots on the floor, his shoes, Gilchrest's shirt. The coach removed Oakley's T-shirt and pressed it against the big kid's nose to stanch the bleeding. As they walked past me toward the office I mumbled an apology to Oakley, but couldn't catch his reply. "You watch your filthy mouth, boy," said Gilchrest to Oakley.

The locker room was unnaturally quiet as I stepped into its steamy atmosphere. Eyes clicked in my direction, looked away. After I was out of my shorts, had my towel wrapped around me, my shower kit in hand, Jack Preston and Brian Nailor approached me. Preston's hair was combed slick and plastic looking. Nailor's stood up like frozen flames. Nailor smiled at me with his big teeth and pale eyes. He poked my arm with a finger. "You fucked up," he said.

"I tried to apologize."

"Won't do you no good," said Preston.

"I swanee," said Nailor.

"It's part of the game," I said. "It was an accident. Wasn't my idea to use volleyballs."

"Don't matter," Preston said. "He's jest lookin for an excuse to fight you."

"I never done nothing to him."

"Don't matter," said Nailor. "He don't like you."

"Brian's right, Clint. He'd jest as soon kill you as look at you."

"I never done nothing to him."

"Look," said Preston, "I know him pretty good. And jest between you and me, it's 'cause you're a city boy—"

"Whadda you mean? I've never—"

"He don't like your clothes—"

"And he don't like the fancy way you talk in class."

"What fancy—"

"I'm tellin him, if you don't mind, Brian."

151

"Tell him then."

"He don't like the way you say 'tennis shoes' instead of sneakers. He don't like coloreds. A whole bunch a things, really."

"I never done nothing to him. He's got no reason—"

"*And*," said Nailor, grinning, "*and*, he says you're a stuck-up rich kid." Nailor's eyes had crow's-feet, bags beneath them. They were a man's eyes.

"My dad's a sergeant," I said.

"You chicken to fight him?" said Nailor.

"Yeah, Clint, don't be chicken. Jest go on and git it over with. He's whupped pert near ever'body else in the class. It ain't so bad."

"Might as well, Oates."

"Yeah, yer pretty skinny, but yer jest about his height. Jest git 'im in a headlock and don't let go."

"Goddamn," I said, "he's got no reason to—"

Their eyes shot right and I looked over my shoulder. Oakley stood at his locker, turning its tumblers. From where I stood I could see that a piece of cotton was wedged up one of his nostrils, and he already had the makings of a good shiner. His acne burned red like a fresh abrasion. He snapped the locker open and kicked his shoes off without sitting. Then he pulled off his shorts, revealing two paddle stripes on his ass. They were fresh red bars speckled with white, the white speckles being the reverse impression of the paddle's suction holes. He must not have watched his filthy mouth while in Gilchrest's presence. Behind me, I heard Preston and Nailor pad to their lockers.

Oakley spoke without turning around. "Somebody's gonna git his skinny black ass kicked, right today, right after school." He said it softly. He slipped his jock off, turned around. I looked away. Out the corner of my eye I saw him stride off, his hairy nakedness a weapon clearing the younger boys from his path. Just before he rounded the corner of the shower stalls, I threw my toilet kit to the floor and stammered, "I—I never did nothing to you, Oakley." He stopped, turned, stepped closer to me, wrapping his towel around himself. Sweat streamed down my rib cage. It felt like ice water. "You wanna go at it right now, boy?"

"I never did nothing to you." I felt tears in my eyes. I couldn't stop them even though I was blinking like mad. "Never."

He laughed. "You busted my nose, asshole."

"What about before? What'd I ever do to you?"

"See you after school, Coonie." Then he turned away, flashing his acne-spotted back like a semaphore. "Why?" I shouted. "Why you wanna fight me?" Oakley stopped and turned, folded his arms, leaned against a toilet stall. "Why you wanna fight *me*, Oakley?" I stepped over the bench. "What'd I do? Why me?" And then unconsciously, as if scratching, as if breathing, I walked toward Marvin, who stood a few feet from Oakley, combing his hair at the mirror. "Why not him?" I said. "How come you're after *me* and not *him*?" The room froze. Froze for a moment that was both evanescent and eternal, somewhere between an eye blink and a week in hell. No one moved, nothing happened; there was no sound at all. And then it was as if all of us at the same moment looked at Marvin. He just stood there, combing away, the only body in motion, I think. He combed his hair and combed it, as if seeing only his image, hearing only his comb scraping his scalp. I knew he'd heard me. There's no way he could not have heard me. But all he did was slide the comb into his pocket and walk out the door.

"I got no quarrel with Marvin," I heard Oakley say. I turned toward his voice, but he was already in the shower.

I was able to avoid Oakley at the end of the school day. I made my escape by asking Mrs. Wickham if I could go to the rest room.

" 'Rest room,' " Oakley mumbled. "It's a damn toilet, sissy."

"Clinton," said Mrs. Wickham. "Can you *not* wait till the bell rings? It's almost three o'clock."

"No ma'am," I said. "I won't make it."

"Well I should make you wait just to teach you to be more mindful about . . . hygiene . . . uh things." She sucked in her cheeks, squinted. "But I'm feeling charitable today. You may go." I immediately left the building, and got on the bus. "Ain't you a little early?" said the bus driver, swinging the door shut. "Just left the office," I said. The driver nodded, apparently not giving me a second thought. I had no idea why I'd told her I'd come from the office, or why she found it a satisfactory answer. Two minutes later the bus filled, rolled, and shook its way to Connolly Air Base. When I got home, my mother was sitting in the living room, smoking her Slims, watching her soap opera. She absently asked me how my day had gone and I told her fine. "Hear from Dad?" I said.

"No, but I'm sure he's fine." She always said that when we hadn't heard from him in a while. I suppose she thought I was worried about him, or that I felt vulnerable without him. It was neither. I just wanted to discuss something with my mother that we both cared about. If I spoke with her about things that happened at school, or on my weekends, she'd listen with half an ear, say something like, "Is that so?" or "You don't say?" I couldn't stand that sort of thing. But when I mentioned my father, she treated me a bit more like an adult, or at least someone who was worth listening to. I didn't want to feel like a boy that afternoon. As I turned from my mother and walked down the hall I thought about the day my father left for Viet Nam. Sharp in his uniform, sure behind his aviator specs, he slipped a cigar from his pocket and stuck it in mine. "Not till I get back," he said. "We'll have us one when we go fishing. Just you and me, out on the lake all day, smoking and casting and sitting. Don't let Mama see it. Put it in y'back pocket." He hugged me, shook my hand, and told me I was the man of the house now. He told me he was depending on me to take good care of my mother and sister. "Don't you let me down, now, hear?" And he tapped his thick finger on my chest. "You almost as big as me. Boy, you something else." I believed him when he told me those things. My heart swelled big enough to swallow my father, my mother, Claire. I loved, feared, and respected myself, my manhood. That day I could have put all of Waco, Texas, in my heart. And it wasn't till about three months later that I discovered I really wasn't the man of the house, that my mother and sister, as they always had, were taking care of me.

For a brief moment I considered telling my mother about what had happened at school that day, but for one thing, she was deep down in the halls of *General Hospital,* and never paid you much mind till it was over. For another thing, I just wasn't the kind of person—I'm still not, really—to discuss my problems with anyone. Like my father I kept things to myself, talked about my problems only in retrospect. Since my father wasn't around I consciously wanted to be like him, doubly like him, I could say. I wanted to be the man of the house in some respect, even if it had to be in an inward way. I went to my room, changed my clothes, and laid out my homework. I couldn't focus on it. I thought about Marvin, what I'd said about him or done to him—I couldn't tell which. I'd done something to him, said something about him; said something about and done something to myself. *How come you're after* me *and not* him? I kept trying to tell myself I hadn't meant it that way. *That* way. I thought about approaching Marvin, telling him what I really meant was that he was more Oakley's age and weight than I. I would tell him I meant I was no match for Oakley. *See, Marvin, what I meant was that he wants to fight a colored guy, but is afraid to fight you 'cause you could beat him.* But try as I did, I couldn't for a moment convince myself that Marvin would believe me. I meant it *that* way and no other. Everybody heard. Everybody knew. That afternoon I forced myself to confront the notion that tomorrow I would probably have to fight both Oakley and Marvin. I'd have to be two men.

I rose from my desk and walked to the window. The light made my skin look orange, and I started thinking about what Wickham had told us once about light. She said that oranges and apples, leaves and flowers, the whole multicolored world, was not what it appeared to be. The colors we see, she said, look like they do only because of the light or ray that shines on them. "The color of the thing isn't what you see, but the light that's reflected off it." Then she shut out the lights and shone a white light lamp on a prism. We watched the pale splay of colors on the projector screen; some people oohed and aahed. Suddenly, she switched on a black light and the color of everything changed. The prism colors vanished, Wickham's arms were purple, the buttons of her dress were as orange as hot coals, rather than the blue they had been only seconds before. We were all very quiet. "Nothing," she said, after a while, "is really what it appears to be." I didn't really understand then. But as I stood at the window, gazing at my orange skin, I wondered what kind of light I could shine on Marvin, Oakley, and me that would reveal us as the same.

I sat down and stared at my arms. They were dark brown again. I worked up a bit of saliva under my tongue and spat on my left arm. I spat again, then rubbed the spittle into it, polishing, working till my arm grew warm. As I spat, and rubbed, I wondered why Marvin did this weird, nasty thing to himself, day after day. Was he trying to rub away the black, or deepen it, doll it up? And if he did this weird nasty thing for a hundred years, would he spit-shine himself invisible, rolling away the eggplant skin, revealing the scarlet muscle, blue vein, pink and yellow tendon, white bone? Then disappear? Seen through, all colors, no colors. Spitting and rubbing. Is this the way you do it? I leaned forward, sniffed the arm. It smelled vaguely of mayonnaise. After an hour or so, I fell asleep.

I saw Oakley the second I stepped off the bus the next morning. He stood outside the gym in his usual black penny loafers,

156

white socks, high-water jeans, T-shirt, and black jacket. Nailor stood with him, his big teeth spread across his bottom lip like playing cards. If there was anyone I felt like fighting, that day, it was Nailor. But I wanted to put off fighting for as long as I could. I stepped toward the gymnasium, thinking that I shouldn't run, but if I hurried I could beat Oakley to the door and secure myself near Gilchrest's office. But the moment I stepped into the gym, I felt Oakley's broad palm clap down on my shoulder. "Might as well stay out here, Coonie," he said. "I need me a little target practice." I turned to face him and he slapped me, one-two, with the back, then the palm of his hand, as I'd seen Bogart do to Peter Lorre in *The Maltese Falcon*. My heart went wild. I could scarcely breathe. I couldn't swallow.

"Call me a nigger," I said. I have no idea what made me say this. All I know is that it kept me from crying. "Call me a nigger, Oakley."

"Fuck you, ya black-ass slope." He slapped me again, scratching my eye. "I don't do what coonies tell me."

"Call me a nigger."

"Outside, Coonie."

"Call me one. Go ahead!"

He lifted his hand to slap me again, but before his arm could swing my way, Marvin Pruitt came from behind me and calmly pushed me aside. "Git out my way, boy," he said. And he slugged Oakley on the side of his head. Oakley stumbled back, stiff-legged. His eyes were big. Marvin hit him twice more, once again to the side of the head, once to the nose. Oakley went down and stayed down. Though blood was drawn, whistles blowing, fingers pointing, kids hollering, Marvin just stood there, staring at me with cool eyes. He spat on the ground, licked his lips, and just stared at me, till Coach Gilchrest and Mr. Calderon tackled him and violently carried him away. He never struggled, never took his eyes off me.

Nailor and Mrs. Wickham helped Oakley to his feet. His already fattened nose bled and swelled so that I had to look away. He looked around, bemused, wall-eyed, maybe scared. It was apparent he had no idea how bad he was hurt. He didn't blink. He didn't even touch his nose. He didn't look like he knew much of anything. He looked at me, looked me dead in the eye, in fact, but didn't seem to recognize me.

That morning, like all other mornings, we said the Pledge of Allegiance, sang "The Yellow Rose of Texas," "The Eyes of Texas Are upon You," and "Mistress Shady." The room stood strangely empty without Oakley, and without Marvin, but at the same time you could feel their presence more intensely somehow. I felt like I did when I'd walk into my mother's room and could smell my father's cigars or cologne. He was more palpable, in certain respects, than when there in actual flesh. For some reason, I turned to look at Ah-so, and just this once I let my eyes linger on her face. She had a very gentle-looking face, really. That surprised me. She must have felt my eyes on her because she glanced up at me for a second and smiled, white teeth, downcast eyes. Such a pretty smile. That surprised me too. She held it for a few seconds, then let it fade. She looked down at her desk, and sat still as a photograph.

LARRY McMURTRY

There Will Be Peace in Korea

About half an hour before dark there was a bad norther struck, but I figured since it was Bud's last night we ought to go someplace anyway. He'd been home two weeks on leave, but we hadn't gone no place—I hadn't even been to see him. Since him and Laveta broke up and we had that fight and Bud put out my eye we hadn't run around much together. I didn't know if he'd want to go nowhere with me, but I thought whether he did or not I'd go over and see him. His Mercury was parked in front of the rooming house—Bud never even had the top up. I parked my pickup behind it and went up on the porch and knocked. I thought Old Lady Mullins never would get to the door. The porch was on the north side of the house and the norther was really singing in off the plains. She finally come and opened the door, but she never unlatched the screen.

"Hello, Miss Mullins," I said. "Bud home?"

"That's his car there, ain't it?" she said. "I guess he's here if he ain't walked off."

She was still dipping snuff. The reason she never asked me in, my Daddy killed himself in one of her rooms. He wasn't even living there, it was my room, but I was off on a rough-necking tower and I guess the room was the best place he could find. Old Lady Mullins hardly ever let me in after that. I wished I'd worn my football jacket—the Levi didn't have no pockets and my hands were about to freeze. Ever time I turned into the wind my eye started watering.

When Bud come to the door he acted kinda surprised but I believe he was glad to see me. Anyhow, he stepped out on the porch. He had on his home clothes, just some Levis and a shirt and his rodeo boots. I didn't know what to say to him.

"Goddamn that wind's getting cold," he said. "Why didn't you come inside?"

"She never unlatched the door," I said. "You know her better than that. I just come by to see what you were doing."

"Nothing," he said. "I was intending to work on my car, but it's turned off too cold."

"I thought we might take off and go someplace," I said. "Maybe to Fort Worth. It might be a good night to drink beer."

"I believe it might," he said. "Only trouble, I got to be back by six in the morning. Bus leaves at six forty-five."

"Aw go get your coat," I said. "We can make that in a walk."

"All right. You might as well get in that pickup and keep warm."

I did, and started the motor. The heater sure felt good. Ever once in awhile the wind would rock the pickup, it was blowing so hard. Some dust was coming with it, too. It wasn't three minutes till Bud came running out. He was a notch smarter than me—he had on his football jacket.

"Wanta go in mine?" he asked. "Might as well get some good out of it."

"Naw, this one's warm and I got a full tank of gas. You might want to sleep on the way back and I'd be afraid to drive yours."

"No reason for you to," he said. "Only trouble, this one's got such a cold back seat. If we was to scare up something we couldn't take advantage of it."

"We could take advantage of it in a motel," I said. I saw Bud was in a good humor and I drove on off. I was glad he felt good—I never intended to fight with Bud nohow. We was best friends all through high school.

"You be over there eighteen months?" I said.

"I reckon." Bud yawned and scratched his cheek. "If I don't get killed first."

We never talked much on the way down. The pickup cab got warm and cozy and Bud had to crack his window to keep from going to sleep. I figured he was thinking about Laveta and all that, but if he was he never brought it up. We had the road to ourselves and the norther for a tail wind besides—I made nearly as good a time as we would have in Bud's Mercury. A cop stopped us outside of Azle, but we didn't offer him any talk and he let us go without a ticket.

"He wasn't so bad," Bud said. "You ought to see them goddam army cops. Meanest bastards on earth."

Pretty soon we crossed Lake Worth and gunned up the hill above the big Convair plant. We topped it, and all the city lights were spread out below us. I always liked to come over that hill. You never get to see that many lights nowhere around Thalia.

"Let's have a beer," I said.

"Let's have about a case."

I pulled off at the first little honky-tonk I came to and we went in and drank a couple of bottles of Pearl. There were some pretty rough-looking old boys working the shuffleboard, so it was probably a good thing Bud didn't wear his army clothes.

161

"This end of town ain't changed," Bud said. "Could get in a fight awful easy out here."

"Or anywhere else," I said. I wished I hadn't. Bud took it wrong and thought I was talking about us.

"Yeah, you can," he said, and stood up.

We went on up the road and hit two or three more beer joints before we decided to head into town. Bud got blue and really swigged down the Pearl.

"Let's hit the south-end," he said. "Then if we don't scare up nothing we can make the Old Jackson."

We went on down to South Main and parked the pickup in front of the Mountaineer Tavern. The wind was blowing right down Main Street about sixty miles an hour, and I mean cold—cold and dusty too, blowing off them old brick streets. There weren't many people moving around. The winos were all in the Mission staying warm. We saw a few country boys standing in front of the Old Jackson with their coat collars turned up. It looked like they just had enough money for one piece of pussy and were flipping to see which one got it. We went into a bar but there didn't no stag women come our way so we just drank a beer and moved on. We went into the Penny Arcade and shot ducks awhile and Bud outshot me eight to five. The man that ran the guns never noticed my eye.

"I ain't been practicing ever day, like you have," I said.

"You ain't gonna have to shoot no goddam Japs, either," he said.

Then we went in a place called the Cozy Inn, where they had a three-piece hillbilly band. It wasn't much of a band and we never paid no attention to the music till the intermission. Then the musicians went off to pee and get themselves a beer and they made the old lady who was working tables go up to the stand and play the guitar while they were gone. I don't know why they made her, because there wasn't but Bud and me and one couple and a few tired-looking old boys at the bar, but when the woman went to singing she sure took a hold of everbody. She was just an ordinary looking old worn-out woman, I guess she musta been fifty years old and Bud said fifty-five, but she could outsing those musicians three to one. She sang "Faded Love" and "Jambalaya," and "Walking the Floor over You," and a couple more I don't remember. She sang like she really meant the words. We all clapped when she quit, and Bud liked her so much he made me go up to the bandstand with him to talk to her. I guess she thought she had sung enough—she was tying her apron on.

"Hello, boys," she said. "What are you'all up to?"

"Oh, trying to find some meanness," Bud said. "Say, my name's Bud Farrow. This is Sonny. Say, I'm going off to Korea tomorrow and sure would like it if you'd sing me another song or two."

"Why I sure will, Bud," she said. "All my boys was in the service. I can't sing but one or two, though—I ain't no regular singer." She grinned at us and picked up her guitar and went back and sat down.

"Folks, these next two songs are for the soldier boys," she said, and that made me feel good because I knew she thought I was in the army too. Only when she got to singing it made me feel pretty bad, because I wasn't in it and Bud was going off anyway. She sang "Dust on the Bible" and "Peace in the Valley," and we all clapped big for her, but then the musicians came back and she handed over the guitar and went to draw some beer.

"Let's get on," I said.

That cold wind hit us right in the face when we stepped out on the street. It felt like it was coming right off the north pole.

"We ain't gonna scare up nothing," Bud said. "Let's go to the Old Jackson."

"I'm game," I said. "I want off this cold-ass street."

We went up and got introduced. Bud's was a little better

looking in the face, but mine was a better size and she was real nice. Her name was Penny. It was a nice place, the Old Jackson—it was warm and had good rugs and about the best beds I ever saw, and nobody gave you any static one way or the other. Only thing, it took a rich man to make it last, and it didn't seem like no time till we were back out in the street, cold as ever.

"Well, how do you feel now?" I asked him.

"Horny," he said. "It was worth the money, though."

"It's right at two o'clock," I said. "We've got two hundred miles to make, we better hit the road."

We hit it, and Bud went right to sleep. He always does that coming back from Fort Worth—I seldom seen him fail. One time when he still had his Chevvy he done it when he was driving and rolled us over three times. It didn't hurt us, but after that I was glad enough to drive and let him sleep. I got to thinking about all the times me and Bud had made that run from Thalia to Fort Worth and back—I guess about a hundred, anyway. We done an awful lot of running around together before we had the fight. Used to, when we were in high school, we'd make it to the Old Jackson about ever three weeks. I wish the damn army had left Bud alone. It was dead enough in Thalia, anyway, without them shipping him off to Korea.

I never slowed down but one time going home. Just this side of Jacksboro I got to needing to pee and stopped and got out. Bud woke up and needed to too so we both turned our backs to the norther and peed on the highway and then got back in and went on. Bud went right back to sleep. The wind was whipping the old pickup all over the road, and I didn't make very good time. But I drove through the stop sign in Thalia just before six and got Bud to his rooming house right on the dot.

"Wake up, Bud," I said. "We're home."

He looked pretty gloopy, but he got out. I slipped in the

house with him and waited while he washed his face and got his army stuff on. He looked a lot different in uniform. He just left most of his other stuff in the room—Old Lady Mullins could put it away if she accidentally found a renter. He put the top up on his Mercury and locked the doors and we went up to the coffee shop and ate some breakfast. Then we drove on over to the drugstore where the bus was supposed to stop, and we waited. We never said much. I knew what Bud was thinking about, but I didn't have no business mentioning it. The wind was blowing paper sacks and sand and once in awhile a tumbleweed across the empty street.

"You don't have to wait if you got some business, Sonny," Bud said. "I can get in the café out of the wind."

"Aw, I got nothing to do this early," I said. "I might as well see you off. Unless you got something you need to do by yourself."

"No, I don't have nothing," Bud said.

Then we seen the Greyhound coming and we got Bud's duffelbag out of the back and stood there in the wind in front of the pickup, waiting for the bus driver to drink his cup of coffee and get his business done in the drugstore. Bud fished around in his pocket and got out both sets of keys to the Mercury and handed them out to me.

"Sonny, you better take care of that car for me," he said. "I was about to go off and forget that. I mean if you don't mind doing it. I may want you to sell it and I may not, I guess I can write and let you know."

"Why I'll be glad to take care of it, Bud," I said. "I can put it in my garage. It don't hurt this old pickup to sit out."

I put the keys in my pocket and Bud picked up his duffelbag.

"I heard it's pussy for the asking over there," I said. "I guess that's one good thing about it."

"Maybe so, if you live to enjoy it," Bud said. "I never did get to ask about you and Laveta."

I had to turn my back on the wind before I could answer him—the wind took my breath.

"Well, I guess it's too bad you never got to go see her, Bud," I said. "Her old man made us get the marriage annulled. He never thought I was rich enough for Laveta, or you either. I think she's going to marry some boy from Dallas."

"I knew she would," Bud said. The wind was so cold it would burn your face, but Bud was looking right into it.

"I think she would have liked to see you," I said. "She never liked getting it annulled no better than I did, at first. I guess she might be liking it a little better now. They sent her off to Dallas to that school."

Bud set his duffelbag down and rubbed his hands together. "I ain't over her yet, Sonny," he said. "After all of this, I ain't over her yet."

"Well, I wish I never had got into it, Bud," I said. "I should have just let you'all make it up."

"Aw, didn't make no difference, he'd of annulled me too," Bud said. "Only I wouldn't a hit you with that bottle, maybe. I never intended to do that. I don't know how come me to do that. Did you'all get to spend the night?"

"Naw we never even done that, Bud. They caught us that night, about ten miles from the J.P.'s. Her old man had the Highway Patrol out looking for us."

"I done that, anyway," he said. "She's a sure sweet girl."

The bus driver came out of the drugstore then and Bud picked up his duffelbag with one hand and me and him shook.

"I enjoyed the visit, Sonny," Bud said. "Watch after this town. I'll see you."

"Bud, take it easy," I said. "I'll be seeing you."

He gave the driver the ticket and got on the bus and it drove away. There wasn't a car on the street, or a person, just that bus. I knew Bud would put off talking about it as long as he could, he always done things that way. I stood there in front of the pickup in the wind, trying to see. A lot of things happened when me and Bud and Laveta was in high school. There were some dust and paper scraps whirling down the street toward me but when the bus was out of sight it seemed like Bud and Laveta were gone for good and I was standing there by myself, in the wind.

TOMÁS RIVERA

Picture of His Father's Face

Translated by Rolando Hinojosa

Nothing to it; all the picture salesmen from San Antonio had to do was to sit and wait, like turkey buzzards, my Pa said, 'cause it was the same every year when the people came back home after some seven months on the migrant trail. There'd be money in their pockets, so, right behind them, the picture salesmen. Nothing to it.

And they brought sample cases of pictures, frames, and black and white and color proofs, too. Here's how they dressed: white shirt first of all, and a tie to go with it. Sure. Respectable, see? And that's why *la raza*, the people, would open their doors to them. I mean, a shirt and a tie represented honesty and respectability. Nothing to it. Easier than stealing, right? . . . and that's what I'm talking about here, see?

You know how people are, how we all of us are wanting

our kids to get ahead and be somebody? Wear a white shirt. And a tie. Sure.

And there they came down those dusty streets, sample cases handy, and they were ready to work the town and the people . . .

Once (and I remember it well, too) I'd gone with Pa on a visit; a call to a compadre's house, when one of the sales types shows up. And he looked hesitant at first, kind of timid. Pa's compadre, Don Mateo, he asked the salesman to come on in, sit, make yourself at home.

"Afternoon (he said), you-all doing all right? We got something new to show you this year. Sí, señor."

"Oh, yeah? And what's that?"

"Let me explain what I'm talking about. You give us a photograph, a picture, right?, and what we do is to amplify it, we make it larger, and that's what amplify means. And then, after that, here's what we do: put that picture on wood. Yes. Sort of rounded off, see? What we call three dimensional."

"And what's the reason for that?"

"Realism. Makes the person come alive, you might say. It-a, it sort of jumps out at you, see? Three dimensional. Here, let me show you this one here . . . This is part of what we do. How about that, eh? Like he's alive, right? It sure looks it, don't it?"

"Yeah, that's pretty good. Hold on a minute, I'm going to show it to my wife . . . (Will you look at this? Isn't that something. Come over here, will you?) . . . You know, we were talking, the wife and me, thinking of sending off some snapshots this year, making them bigger. Enlarging them, right? Ah . . . but this ought to cost quite a bit, am I right?"

"Not as much as you'd think. The problem is *the process,* do you know what I mean by that?"

"Ah-hah. How much money we talking about here?"

"Well, not as much as you'd think, like I said. How does thirty dollars sound? But first-class, rounded off, see? Three dimensional . . ."

"Well, thirty dollars does sound kind of steep to me. I thought I heard you say it wouldn't go much more than the old ones. And this is on the installment plan, you say?"

"Well, if it was up to me . . . but it happens that we got us a new sales supervisor this year, and with him, it's cash; cash on the barrelhead, I'm afraid. You know how it is, but he's also right in a way, see? It's good, first class, quality workmanship. It'd make a great picture for that table, see? Realer than real. Rounded off, like this one here. Here, hold it yourself. Fine work, right? And we can do it in a month, too. Everything. But what we need from you is to tell us what color clothing, hair, and like that; and then, before you know it, the month's gone by, and you got yourselves the genuine article here. For a lifetime. And listen to this: we'll throw in the frame, too. Free, gratis. And it'll take a month. Tops. And I wish we could do business, but this new supervisor, he wants to get paid on the nail. And he pushes us, see?"

"Oh, I like the work, all right. But it's the money; it's kind-a high."

"I know what you mean. But you got to agree that that's what we call first class goods, substantial, see? . . . and that's what we're looking at here. You never seen work like this in your life, am I right? On wood? Like that?"

"No, I sure haven't, but . . . here, I'll ask the wife again . . . What do you think, eh?"

"It's nice. I like it. A lot. Look, why don't we try one? See how it comes out. We like it, we get some more. Let's start off with Chuy's picture. That's the only one we got of him, though, God rest him . . ."

"She's right. We took it right here before he left for Korea; and he died there. See? Here's the picture we're talking about. You, ah, you think you can do that rounding off with this one? Like you say? Like he looks alive, kind of?"

"Absolutely. We do a lot of servicemen, yes ma'am. You see, in this rounding that we do, they're better than photographs or snapshots. A whole lot. Now, all I need's the size, but you got to tell me that; the size you want. Oh, and that free frame I talked about, you want it in a square shape? Round, maybe? What d'you say? What should I write down here?"

(Don Mateo looked at his wife) "What d'you think? Can we order the one?"

"Well, I already told you what I think. I'd like to have my boy looking like that. Rounded off, in color."

"Okay, write it up like that, but like I said: that's the only picture we got of the boy. So, you got to take good care of it. He was supposed to send us one in uniform, all fitted out, see? And with the Mexican and the United States flags around him. You seen 'em, right? But we never got that picture. What happened was that as soon as he got to Korea, we then heard from the government. Missing in action, they said. Missing. So you best take good care a-that photo there."

"We'll take good care of it, yessir. You can count on it. The company knows you all are making a sacrifice here; oh, yes. We don't want you to worry none. And you just wait when you get it back, cleaned up and everything. What's it gonna be? We put on a navy-blue uniform on 'im?"

"Can you really do that? He's not even wearing a uniform on this one."

"Nothing to it. We just kind of fix it in; what we call an *inlay* job. You know about that? On the wood, see? Here, let me show you these over here . . . See this one here? Well, that boy there didn't have no uniform on when they took his picture. Our company was the one that put it on him. How about that, eh? Blue is it? Navy-blue?"

"Oh yeah, sure."

"And don't you worry none about your boy's picture, okay?"

"How long till we get those pictures, you think?"

"Can't be too long, right? But it takes time on account of

the process. It's good work. And these people sure know what they're doing, too. You notice? The people in the samples looked alive, real."

"Oh, yeah, I know they do good work, no denying that. It's just that it's been over a month, or more."

"Yeah, but don't forget: how many towns between here and San Antonio? They must've gone through every one, see? It'll probably take 'em more'n a month on account of all the business they did."

"Yeah, that's got to be it, then. Sure."

And then, two weeks after that last exchange, something happened. There'd been some hard rains in the region, and some kids fooling around near the city dump, over by those big drain pipes there, well, that's where the kids found the photographs! Wet, and most beyond recognition, worn out, through and through, and full of holes some of them. But they were the snapshots and the pictures, all right. You could see they were; most of them were the same size, and you could still make out some of the faces on them, too.

Sold! They'd been taken in, and that sure didn't take long to sink in. Taken. Like babies. And Pa's compadre, Don Mateo, he got so mad, so mad, he just took off to San Antonio; went after that guy who'd conned them good, who'd taken their money, who'd taken his Chuy's last picture.

"Well, Compadre, I'll tell you what I did; how I went about it. First off, I stayed with Esteban. Every morning I'd go out with him, to that stall of his, where he sells vegetables; the San Antonio *mercado,* that open-air veg market. Worked with him, loading and unloading, helping out, you know. But I had me a plan, a hunch; a hope, maybe. And I just knew I was going to run across that big city con man, yeah.

"Anyway, every morning after helping Esteban set up that stand of his, I'd walk around some of the barrios there, by the market. Got to see a lot, see? But by now, it wasn't the money so much. That mad kind-of wore off. It was the wife's crying, see? And that'd been Chuy's one and only picture, and we'd told the guy, too. The only one we had of him, and the wife crying all the time. So it wasn't the money so much, now. Oh, we'd found them all there in the sewers, but that snapshot was ruined. Nothing left, see?"

"But in San Antonio, Compadre? How would anyone go about finding a guy like that?"

"I'll make it short, Compadre. He himself showed up at Esteban's stall one day. Just like that! Bought himself some vegetables, he did, right there. And I saw him face to face. He saw me too, but he made out like he didn't know me, know who I was. Never seen me before, see? Oh, I made him right away, and then you know what happened? Let me say this, Compadre, when you're angry, really angry, but I mean really angry now, you don't forget a face or anything. It all comes clear somehow.

"Well, I came up to him, grabbed him, yeah I did, and he went *white* on me, scared. You bet, he was. And I said: 'I want my boy's picture. And I want it rounded off, like you said. Three di—mension. You got that?'

"And then I told him I'd eat him up and spit him out if he didn't come through with that portrait of his. Hmph. He didn't know what to do, where to start. But he did it. From memory, you understand? But he did it."

"Yeah? Well how did he do that, Compadre?"

"Well, that's a mystery, but with fear working overtime, I guess you might say you can remember *anything,* everything. And there it was, three days later, and I didn't have to go after him this time. There he was at Esteban's stall, picture and everything. Well, there it is, see it? Right behind you. Good piece of work, right?"

"Tell you the truth, Compadre, I can't remember what young Chuy looked like anymore . . . But he, ah, he was beginning to look like you, wasn't he?"

"He sure was, Compadre. And you know what people say when they see the picture? They say the same thing. Yeah. That Chuy, had my boy lived, he'd look a lot like me, they say. And there's the picture, here, let me get it for you. I—dentical, eh, Compadre? Him and me, right?"

★

ANNETTE SANFORD

Trip in a Summer Dress

Moths are already dying under the street lamps when I board the bus. I have said goodbye to my mother and to Matthew who is crying because he's almost six and knows I won't be back in time for his birthday. I won't be back for the next one either, but who's going to tell him that?

I spread myself out on two seats. I have a brown plastic purse, a tan makeup case, and a paperback book. I could be anybody starting a trip.

The driver is putting the rest of my things in the luggage compartment. His name is E. E. Davis, and the sign at the front of the bus says not to talk to him. He can count on me.

The bus is coughing gray smoke into the loading lanes. I can see my mother and Matthew moving back into the station, out of sight. I fan myself with the paperback and smooth the skirt of my dress. Blue. Cotton. No sleeves.

"It's too late for a summer dress," my mother said while we waited. Before that, she said October is a cold month in Arkansas. She said that Matthew needs vitamins, that the man who sells tickets looks like Uncle Harry. Some things she said twice without even noticing.

We're moving finally.

E. E. Davis is making announcements in a voice like a spoon scraping a cooking pot. *We rest twenty minutes in Huntsville, we stay in our seats while the coach is in motion.* All the time he's talking I'm watching my mother and Matthew on the corner waiting for the light to change. Matthew is sucking two fingers and searching the bus windows for me. I could wave, but I don't.

I'm riding off into the night because two days from now in Eureka Springs, Arkansas, I'm going to be married. Bill Richards is his name. He has brown hair and a gentle touch and a barbershop. He thinks marriages are made in heaven. He thinks Matthew is my mother's son.

She's young enough. She married and had her first child when she was fifteen. So did I, but I wasn't married.

Matthew was born on Uncle Harry's tree farm in East Texas where I went with my mother after she told all her friends she was pregnant again. She needed fresh air and a brother's sympathy, she said, and me to look after her.

I was skinny and flat-chested and worked after school in the aviary at the zoo mixing up peanut butter and sunflower seeds and feeding fuzzy orphans with an eyedropper. Most nights I studied. What happened was just a mistake I made because I'd never given much thought to that kind of thing and when the time came it caught me without my mind made up one way or the other.

So we went to the tree farm.

Every day while we waited my mother preached me a sermon: you didn't pass around a child like a piece of cake, and you didn't own him like a house or a refrigerator, and you didn't tell him one thing was true one day and something else was true the next. You took a child and set him down in the safest place you could find. Then you taught him the rules and let him grow. One thing for sure: you didn't come along later just when he was thinking he was a rose and tell him he was a violet instead, just because it suited you to.

What you did was you gave him to your mother and father and you called him your brother and that was that.

Except for one thing. They let you name him.

I picked Matthew because of the dream.

All through the night I'd been Moses' sister tending to the reed basket when the queen found him. All night I was Moses' sister running up and down that river bank hollering till my throat about burst. When the pain was over, there he was—with my mother taking care of him just like the Bible story says. Only you can't name a little pink baby Moses because Moses was mostly an old man. So I settled on Matthew.

It made him mine.

There are four people on this bus. There's a black boy in the second seat blowing bubbles with his gum. Across from him are a couple of ladies just out of the beauty parlor with hair too blue, and a child one seat up across from me. A little girl. Scared probably. She's pretty young for traveling in the dark.

I'm not going to look at them anymore. Everything you do in this life gets mixed up with something else, so you better watch out, even just looking at people. Landscapes are safer.

Pine trees, rice fields, oil rigs. I got my fill of them coming back from Uncle Harry's. I didn't look once at Matthew, but I felt him, even when he wasn't crying. He had hold of me way down deep and wouldn't let go for love nor money.

I sat on the back seat. My father drove and my mother cooed at her brand-new son, the first one in four girls. If she said that one time, she said it a hundred.

Finally *I* said—so loud my father ran off the road, "He's not *your* child! I birthed him. I'm his mother, and I'm going to raise him up to know I am! Now what's the matter with that?"

My mother said, "Count the I's, and you'll know." She didn't even turn around.

I got used to it, the way you do a thorn that won't come out or chronic appendicitis. But it's hard to pretend all the time that something's true when it isn't.

So I didn't.

I talked to Matthew about it. I fed him cereal on the back porch by the banana tree, and I told him just how it was he came about. I took him to the park in his red-striped stroller and showed him pansies and tulips and iris blooming. I told him they were beautiful and that's the way it is with love.

Only I hadn't loved his father, I said, and that's where I was wrong. A person ought never to give his body if his soul can't come along.

I told him I'd never leave him because he was me and I was him, and no matter what his mother—who was really his grandmother—said, I had a plan that would save us.

Then he learned to talk, and I had to quit all that.

It's just as well 'cause look at me now. Leaving. Going away from him as hard and fast as ever I can. Me and E. E. Davis burning up the pavement to Huntsville so we can rest twenty minutes and start up again.

Now here's a town.

That little girl across the aisle is rising up and squirming around. Maybe she lives here. Maybe one of those houses going by with lights on and people eating supper inside is hers. But I'm not going to ask. You get a child started talking, you can't stop them sometimes.

Like Matthew.

The day I said yes to Bill Richards I set my plan a-going. I took Matthew to the park like I always had. We sat under a tree where I knew something was likely to happen because lately it always did, and when it started, I said, "Looka there, Matthew. See that redbird feeding her baby?"

"That's not her baby," he said when he finally found the limb. "She's littler than it."

"That's right. The baby's a cowbird, but it *thinks* it's a redbird."

He was real interested. "Does the redbird know it's not her baby?"

"Yes, but she keeps on taking care of it because it hatched in her nest and she loves it."

"How did it get in her nest?"

"Its mama left it there." I was taking it slow by then, being mighty careful. "She gave it to the redbirds, but just for a little while."

Matthew looked at me. "Mamas don't do that."

"Sometimes they do. If they have to."

"Why would they have to?"

"If they can't take care of the babies, it's better that way."

"Why can't they take care of them?"

"Well. For one thing, cowbirds are too lazy to build nests. Or won't. Or can't." I saw right away I'd said it all wrong.

Matthew stuck out his bottom lip. "I don't like cowbirds."

"They aren't really bad birds," I said quick as I could. "They just got started on the wrong foot—*wing*." Nothing went right with that conversation.

"They're ugly too."

"The mama comes back, Matthew. She always comes back. She whistles and the baby hears and they fly away together."

"I wouldn't go. I'd peck her with my nose."

"Let's go look at the swans," I said.

"I'd tell her to go away and never come back."

"Maybe you'd like some popcorn."

"I would be a redbird forever!"

"Or peanuts. How about a nice big bag?"

When we got home he crawled up in my mother's lap and

kissed her a million times. He told her cowbirds are awful. He told her he was mighty glad he belonged to her and not to a cowbird. She was mighty glad too, she said.

I told her now was the time to set things straight and she could be a plenty big help if she wanted to.

She told me little pitchers have big ears.

Eureka Springs is about the size of this town we're going through. In Eureka Springs the barbershop of Bill Richards is set on a mountain corner, he says, and the streets drop off like shelves around it. Eureka Springs is a tourist place. Christ stands on a hill there and sees the goings-on. In Eureka Springs, Bill Richards has a house with window boxes in the front and geraniums growing out, just waiting for someone to pick them.

I can see people in these houses in this town hanging up coats and opening doors and kissing each other. Women are washing dishes, and kids are getting lessons.

Next year Matthew is going to school in Houston. My mother will walk with him to the corner where he'll catch the bus. He'll have on short pants and a red shirt because red's his favorite color, and he won't want to let go of her hand. In Eureka Springs it will be too cool for a boy to start school wearing short pants.

In Eureka Springs, a boy won't have to.

I can see I was wrong about that little girl. She's not scared. She's been up and down the aisle twice and pestered E. E. Davis. She's gotten chewing gum from the boy and candy from the ladies. It's my turn now, I guess.

"Hello." I know better, but I can't help it.

She puts a sticky hand on my arm. "How come you're crying?"

"Dirt in my eye."

"From the chemical plant," she says, pretty smarty. "They're p'luters. They make plastic bags and umber-ellas."

I open my purse and take out a Kleenex. "How do you know?"

"I know everything on this road."

"You live on it?"

She throws back her head like a TV star. "Prac'ly. Fridays I go that way." She points toward the back window. "Sundays I come back. My daddy's got week-in custardy."

She hangs on the seat in front of me and breathes through her mouth. She smells like corn chips. "They had a big fight, but Mama won most of me. You got any kids?"

"No—yes."

"Don't you know?" A tooth is missing under those pouty lips.

"I have a boy, a little younger than you." I never said it out loud before to anybody but Matthew, and him when he was a baby.

"Where is he?"

"At home. With his grandmother."

"Whyn't you bring him?"

"I'm going a far piece. He's better off there."

She pops her gum and swings a couple of times on one heel. "You got a boyfriend?"

"Yes." It's out before I can stop it. I ought to bite my tongue off or shake her good. A child with no manners is an abomination before the Lord, my mother says. That's one thing about my mother. She won't let Matthew get away with a thing.

The child turns up her mouth corners, but it's not a smile. "My mama's got one too. Name's Rex. He's got three gold teeth and a Cadillac."

"How far is it to Huntsville?"

"Two more towns and a dance hall."

"You run on. I'm going to take a nap."

She wanders off up the aisle and plops in a seat. In a second her feet are up in it, her skirt sky-high. Somebody ought to care that she does that. Somebody ought to be here to tell her to sit up like a lady. Especially on a bus. All kinds of people ride buses.

I met Bill Richards on a bus. Going to Galveston for Splash Day. He helped us off and carried my tote bag and bought us hot dogs. He bought Matthew a snow cone. He built him a castle. He gave him a shoulder ride right into the waves. A girl married to Bill Richards wouldn't have to do a thing but love him.

A girl married to Bill Richards wouldn't tell him she had a son with no father, my mother said. And she wouldn't tell her son he was her son. Or a redbird either. She would forget it and love her brother.

We're stopping at a filling station sort of place. The blue-haired ladies are tying nets around their heads and stuffing things in paper sacks. They get out and a lot of hot air comes in. The door pops shut and E. E. Davis gives it the gas. "Ten more miles to Huntsville."

"My mama better be there this time!" the child says, loud and quivery. I had it right in the first place, I guess. Her scare is just all slicked over with chewing gum and smart talk. Inside she's powerful shaky.

"Your mama'll be there, don't you worry." Before I can close my mouth she's on me like a plaster cast. I should have been a missionary.

"She's always late. Last time I waited all night. The bus station man bought me a cheese sandwich and covered me up with his coat."

"Something kept her, I guess."

"Yeah." She slides down in the seat beside me. "Rex."

I don't want to talk to her. I want to think about things. I want to figure out how it's going to be in Eureka Springs with Christ looking right in the kitchen window when I'm kissing Bill Richards, and Him knowing all the time about Moses' sister. I want to think about Matthew growing up and getting married himself and even dying without ever knowing I'm his mother.

Most of all I want to get off this bus and go and get my baby.

"Huntsville!" yells E. E.

"I told you! I told you she wouldn't be here." That child's got a grip on my left hand so tight the blood's quit running. We're standing in the waiting room with lots of faces, but none of them is the right one. It's pitch dark outside and hot as a devil's poker.

"Just sit down," I say. "She'll come."

"I have to go to the bathroom."

"Go ahead. I'll watch for her."

I go in the phone booth. No matter what my mother says, Matthew is a big boy. He can take it. So can Bill Richards. I put two quarters and seven nickels on the shelf by the receiver. I get the dial tone. I spin the numbers out, eleven of them, and drop my money in the slot.

I see the woman coming in out of the dark. She's holding hands with a gold-toothed man and her mouth's all pouty like the child's. My mother's voice shouts hello in my ear.

"Wait," I tell her.

I open the door of the phone booth. "Wait! She's in the restroom. Your child. There, she's coming yonder."

I can see they wish she wasn't. I can see how they hate Sundays.

"Talk if you're going to," my mother says. She only calls long distance when somebody dies.

"Mama, I wanted to tell you—"

"That you wish you had your coat. I knew it! The air's too still and sticky not to be breeding a blizzard."

"It's *hot* here, for goodness sakes!"

"Won't be for long. Thirty by morning the TV says. Twenty where you're going. Look in the makeup case. I stuck in your blue wool sweater."

"Matthew—"

"In bed and finally dropping off. I told him an hour ago, the sooner you shed today, the quicker tomorrow'll come, but he's something else to convince, that boy."

"Comes by it naturally," I say, and plenty loud, but she doesn't hear.

"Have a good trip," she's yelling, "and wrap up warm in the wind."

When I step outside, it's blowing all right, just like she said. Hard from the north and sharp as scissors.

By the time E. E. Davis swings open the door and bellows "All aboard for Eureka Springs," that wind is tossing up news-papers and bus drivers' caps and hems of summer dresses. It's whipping through door cracks and rippling puddles and freez-ing my arms where the sleeves ought to be.

If I was my mother, I'd get mighty tired of always being right.

C. W. SMITH

Witnesses

Norma should tell this story, but I don't think she will. So I have to do my best, though I might not tell it exactly as it happened. My story is this. Norma called me to say that her friend Patsy had died. I'd met Patsy once when she'd come to Dallas to collaborate with Norma on a book about quilting.

I told Norma I was sorry to hear about Patsy. "I know you must be devastated," I said. "You were friends for such a long time."

Yes, said Norma. "Since we were twelve." They'd grown up in New Mexico together, got married and divorced in tandem, stayed cross-continental pen pals for forty years. Patsy, childless, was godmother to Norma's daughter.

Was it cancer?

"Her heart exploded," said Norma.

You know Patsy, she went on, how she kept really fit and ran three miles a day—.

It was like Jim Fixx? No warning at all?

"Well, she'd had a leaky heart." A congenital condition. The doctors had told her she was at risk in jogging, "but she wanted to take care of her problem this way." And she'd been doing fine.

It happened while she was running?

No, it was like this. Patsy was coming out of a supermarket. She was carrying a bag of groceries in her arms. A woman walking into the store happened to look at Patsy's face and saw her eyes roll back. She realized Patsy was passing out, so she stepped right up to Patsy and hugged her. The woman struggled to hold Patsy upright until a second woman, then a third, saw what was needed and rushed over to help the first woman lay Patsy back onto the floor. The second woman took off her gray cardigan, folded it, and slipped it under Patsy's head. While the third retrieved cans of cat food that had spilled from Patsy's sack, the first woman told a checker to call an ambulance. She pressed her fingers to Patsy's wrist but didn't feel a pulse. A fourth woman with wild red hair and paint-dabbed jeans went to her knees, loosened Patsy's concho belt, then blew into her mouth, over and over, and massaged her chest. Meanwhile, the second woman looked into Patsy's purse and located her home phone number, but when she went and called it, of course all she got was Patsy's machine. With nothing left to do, the other three knelt beside the woman doing CPR and waited.

The paramedics arrived but couldn't bring Patsy back. When they had put her on a stretcher and slid her into the ambulance, the first woman took out a business card, wrote on the back of it, and slipped it inside Patsy's purse, which the red-haired woman was holding. She in turn put the purse into the ambulance, and the third woman sat the groceries by Patsy's side.

*   *   *

The first woman's name is April Yuan, and she is a buyer for an import firm. When the ambulance left, she and the other three women stood at the curb for a minute, not knowing what to do. April Yuan had gone into the store to buy panty hose because she had a 2:30 meeting, and it was already three o'clock. The second woman draped her gray cardigan over her forearm and stroked it as you might a cat.

The other woman who had helped lay Patsy back, who had retrieved Patsy's cat food and had put Patsy's groceries in the ambulance, said, Well, I've got to go back to work now. It's a day-care center, couple blocks up that way. She looked to April Yuan and the others as if for permission to leave, and they shrugged and murmured that they understood. But then the day-care worker, a care-giver, made no move to go. The woman with the cardigan said, "I'm just visiting Berkeley, and I don't know anyone here." The woman who had tried CPR said, "I need to sit down and have some tea." The visitor with the cardigan looked relieved and said, "Me too."

They all four walked down the street a way until they came to a cafe none had ever been inside. The tables were of plywood with glossy, lacquered tops, and the menu said, We serve no caffeinated beverages. April Yuan, who has since been back to the place twice with Rachel, said the lunch crowd had cleared out. The place was quiet and empty but for one waitress who was wiping tables with a natural sponge the size of a bread loaf.

The four women ordered orange-cinnamon tea. The waitress brought a teapot with a blue glaze and four matching mugs on a tray. Then after a moment the waitress brought, unasked, fresh hot blueberry muffins for them to sample free. They didn't talk much at first. The red-haired woman lifted her mug high enough to peer at the bottom of it. Somebody said, "Poor woman." The visitor's hands were trembling, so her tea got cold before she could drink it. The red-haired woman said this was the only time she'd ever used her CPR training, and the others said don't feel bad—it was good that you tried, it was more than we did. The woman who worked at the day-care center asked, "I wonder if she had children?" April Yuan had noticed Patsy had no wedding ring.

They stayed for about an hour. The funny thing was, said April Yuan later, "We didn't talk about your friend Patsy very long." They didn't know what to say about what had happened. They all talked for a while about being parents and having them. The visitor with the cardigan said she had two teenage sons back home in Michigan. April Yuan has a grown daughter, but she told the others only about her mother, who has Alzheimer's. Then the visitor from Michigan asked the day-care woman how she put her hair in those corn rows. It takes days, answered the other. You got to wait until you want to punish yourself. They all laughed. They talked about the tea, the crockery. After a bit, April Yuan got up to go call her husband even though she knew he was busy at work, and when she came back to the table, the others were standing over the bill and chatting while they dug change out of their purses and pockets.

April was the last to leave the cafe. The woman with the teenage sons was already striding far up the street. A breeze had come up while they were in the cafe, and, while walking, the woman slipped her cardigan over her shoulders. Beside her, the day-care worker was gesturing in a way that meant giving directions. When the two reached the corner, they both looked back and waved good-bye. Then they disappeared.

The red-haired woman in the paint-smeared jeans had been lagging behind, letting the other two outpace her. She stopped and waited for April to catch up to her. "I'm Rachel," she said, and stuck out her hand. "I saw what you wrote on that card about being with her when she died. I hope someone from the family calls you."

LYNNA WILLIAMS

Personal Testimony

The last night of church camp, 1963, and I am sitting in the front row of the junior mixed-voice choir looking out on the crowd in the big sanctuary tent. The tent glows, green and white and unexpected, in the Oklahoma night; our choir director, Dr. Bledsoe, has schooled us in the sudden crescendos needed to compete with the sounds cars make when their drivers cut the corner after a night at the bars on Highway 10 and see the tent rising out of the plain for the first time. The tent is new to Faith Camp this year, a gift to God and the Southern Baptist Convention from the owner of a small circus who repented, and then retired, in nearby Oklahoma City. It is widely rumored among the campers that Mr. Talliferro came to Jesus late in life, after having what my mother would call Life Experiences. Now he walks through camp with the unfailing good humor of a man who, after years of begging hard-

scrabble farmers to forsake their fields for an afternoon of ele-
phants and acrobats, has finally found a real draw: his weekly
talks to the senior boys on "Sin and the Circus" incorporate a
standing-room-only question-and-answer period, and no one
ever leaves early.

Although I know I will never be allowed in the tent to
hear one of Mr. Talliferro's talks—I will not be twelve forever,
but I will always be a girl—I am encouraged by his late arrival
into our Fellowship of Believers. I will take my time, too, I
think: first I will go to high school, to college, to bed with a
boy, to New York. (I think of those last two items as one since,
as little as I know about sex, I do know it is not something I
will ever be able to do in the same time zone as my mother.)
Then when I'm fifty-two or so and have had, like Mr. Talliferro, sufficient Life Experiences, I'll move back to west Texas
and repent.

Normally, thoughts of that touching—and distant—scene
of repentance are how I entertain myself during evening worship service. But tonight I am unable to work up any enthusiasm for the vision of myself sweeping into my hometown to Be
Forgiven. For once my thoughts are entirely on the worship
service ahead.

My place in the choir is in the middle of six other girls
from my father's church in Fort Worth; we are dressed alike in
white lace-trimmed wash-and-wear blouses from J. C. Penney
and modest navy pedal pushers that stop exactly three inches
from our white socks and tennis shoes. We are also alike in having mothers who regard travel irons as an essential accessory to
Christian Young Womanhood; our matching outfits are, there-
fore, neatly ironed.

At least their outfits are. I have been coming to this camp
in the southwestern equivalent of the Sahara Desert for six
years now, and I know that when it is a hundred degrees at sun-
set, cotton wilts. When I used my iron I did the front of my
blouse and the pants, so I wouldn't stand out, and trusted that

anyone standing behind me would think I was wrinkled from the heat.

Last summer, or the summer before, when I was still riding the line that separates good girls from bad, this small deception would have bothered me. This year I am twelve and a criminal. Moral niceties are lost on me. I am singing "Just as I Am" with the choir and I have three hundred dollars in my white Bible, folded and taped over John 3:16.

Since camp started three weeks ago, I have operated a business in the arts and crafts cabin in the break between afternoon Bible study and segregated (boys only/girls only) swimming. The senior boys, the same ones who are learning critical new information from Mr. Talliferro every week, are paying me to write the personal testimonies we are all expected to give at evening worship service.

We do not dwell on personal motivation in my family. When my brother, David, and I sin, it is the deed my parents talk about, not mitigating circumstances, and the deed they punish. This careful emphasis on what we do, never on why we do it, has affected David and me differently. He is a good boy, endlessly kind and cheerful and responsible, but his heroes are not the men my father followed into the ministry. David gives God and our father every outward sign of respect, but he worships Clarence Darrow and the law. At fifteen, he has been my defense lawyer for years.

While David wants to defend the world, I am only interested in defending myself. I know exactly why I have started the testimony business: I am doing it to get back at my father. I am doing it because I am adopted.

Even though I assure my customers with every sale that we will not get caught, I never write a testimony without imagining public exposure of my wrongdoing. The scene is so familiar to me that I do not have to close my eyes to see it: the summons to the camp director's office and the door closing behind

193

me; the shocked faces of other campers when the news leaks out; the Baptist Academy girls who comb their hair and go in pairs, bravely, to offer my brother comfort; the automatic rotation of my name to the top of everyone's prayer list. I spend hours imagining the small details of my shame, always leading to the moment when my father, called from Fort Worth to take me home, arrives at camp.

That will be my moment. I have done something so terrible that even my father will not be able to keep it a secret. I am doing this because of my father's secrets.

We had only been home from church for a few minutes; it was my ninth birthday, and when my father called me to come downstairs to his study, I was still wearing the dress my mother had made for the occasion, pink dotted swiss with a white satin sash. David came out of his room to ask me what I had done this time—he likes to be prepared for court—but I told him not to worry, that I was wholly innocent of any crime in the weeks just before my birthday. At the bottom of the stairs I saw my mother walk out of the study and knew I was right not to be concerned: in matters of discipline my mother and father never work alone. At the door it came to me: my father was going to tell me I was old enough to go with him now and then to churches in other cities. David had been to Atlanta and New Orleans and a dozen little Texas towns; my turn had finally come.

My father was standing by the window. At the sound of my patent-leather shoes sliding across the hardwood floor, he turned and motioned for me to sit on the sofa. He cleared his throat; it was a sermon noise I had heard hundreds of times, and I knew that he had prepared whatever he was going to say.

All thoughts of ordering room-service hamburgers in an Atlanta hotel left me—prepared remarks meant we were dealing with life or death or salvation—and I wished for my mother and David. My father said, "This is hard for your mother; she wanted to be here, but it upsets her so, we thought I should talk to you alone." We had left territory I knew, and I sat up straight to listen, as though I were still in church.

My father, still talking, took my hands in his; after a moment I recognized the weight of his Baylor ring against my skin as something from my old life, the one in which I had woken up that morning a nine-year-old, dressed for church in my birthday dress, and come home.

My father talked and talked and talked; I stopped listening. I had grown up singing about the power of blood. I required no lengthy explanation of what it meant to be adopted. It meant I was not my father's child. It meant I was a secret, even from myself.

In the three years since that day in my father's study, I have realized, of course, that I am not my mother's child, either. But I have never believed that she was responsible for the lie about my birth. It is my father I blame. I am not allowed to talk about my adoption outside my family ("It would only hurt your mother," my father says. "Do you want to hurt your mother?"). Although I am universally regarded by the women of our church as a Child Who Wouldn't Know a Rule If One Reached Up and Bit Her in the Face, I do keep this one. My stomach hurts when I even think about telling anyone, but it hurts, too, when I think about having another mother and father somewhere. When the pain is enough to make me cry, I try to talk to my parents about it, but my mother's face changes even before I can get the first question out, and my father always follows her out of the room. "You're our child," he says when he returns. "We love you, and you're ours."

I let him hug me, but I am thinking that I have never heard my father tell a lie before. I am not his child. Not in the way David is, not in the way I believed I was. Later I remember that lie and decide that all the secrecy is for my father's benefit, that he is ashamed to tell the world that I am not his child because he is ashamed of me. I think about the Ford my father bought in Dallas three years ago; it has never run right, but he will not take it back. I think about that when I am sitting in my bunk with a flashlight, writing testimonies to the power of God's love.

My father is one reason I am handcrafting Christian testimonies while my bunkmates are making place mats from Popsicle sticks. There is another reason: I'm good at it.

Nothing else has changed. I remain Right Fielder for Life in the daily softball games. The sincerity of my belief in Jesus is perennially suspect among the most pious, and most popular, campers. And I am still the only girl who, in six years of regular attendance, has failed to advance even one step in Girls' Auxiliary. (Other, younger girls have made it all the way to Queen Regent with Scepter, while I remain a perpetual Lady-in-Waiting.) Until this year, only the strength of my family connections has kept me from sinking as low in the camp hierarchy as Cassie Mosley, who lisps and wears colorful native costumes that her missionary parents send from Africa.

I arrived at camp this summer as I do every year, resigned and braced to endure but buoyed by a fantasy life that I believe is unrivaled among twelve-year-old Baptist girls. But on our second night here, the promise of fish sticks and carrot salad hanging in the air, Bobby Dunn came and stood behind me in the cafeteria line.

Bobby Dunn, blond, ambitious, and in love with Jesus, is Faith Camp's standard for male perfection. He is David's friend, but he has spoken to me only once, on the baseball field last year, when he suggested that my unhealthy fear of the ball was really a failure to trust God's plan for my life. Since that day I have taken some comfort in noticing that Bobby Dunn follows the Scripture reading by moving his finger along the text.

Feeling him next to me, I took a breath, wondering if Bobby, like other campers in other years, had decided to attempt to bring me to a better understanding of what it means to serve Jesus. But he was already talking, congratulating me on my testimony at evening worship service the night before. (I speak publicly at camp twice every summer, the exact number required by some mysterious formula that allows me to be left alone the rest of the time.)

"You put it just right," he said. "Now me, I know what I want to say, but it comes out all wrong. I've prayed about it, and it seems to be God wants me to do better."

He looked at me hard, and I realized it was my turn to say something. Nothing came to me, though, since I agreed with him completely. He does suffer from what my saintly brother, after one particularly gruesome revival meeting, took to calling Jesus Jaw, a malady that makes it impossible for the devoted to say what they mean and sit down. Finally I said what my mother says to the ladies seeking comfort in the Dorcas Bible class: "Can I help?" Before I could take it back, Bobby Dunn had me by the hand and was pulling me across the cafeteria to a table in the far corner.

The idea of my writing testimonies for other campers—a sort of ghostwriting service for Jesus, as Bobby Dunn saw it—was Bobby's, but before we got up from the table, I had refined it and made it mine. The next afternoon in the arts and crafts cabin I made my first sale: five dollars for a two-minute testimony detailing how God gave Michael Bush the strength to stop swearing. Bobby was shocked when the money changed hands—I could see him thinking, Temple. Moneylenders. Jeesus!—but Michael Bush is the son of an Austin car dealer, and he quoted his earthly father's scripture: "You get what you pay for."

Michael, who made me a professional writer with money he earned polishing used station wagons, is a sweet, slow-talking athlete from Bishop Military School. He'd been dateless for months and was convinced it was because the Baptist Academy girls had heard that he has a tendency to take the Lord's

197

name in vain on difficult fourth downs. After his testimony that night, Michael left the tent with Patsy Lewis, but he waved good night to me.

For an underground business, I have as much word-of-mouth trade from the senior boys as I can handle. I estimate that my volume is second only to that of the snack stand that sells snow cones. Like the snow-cone stand, I have high prices and limited hours of operation. I arrive at the arts and crafts cabin every day at 2:00 P.M., carrying half-finished pot holders from the day before, and senior boys drift in and out for the next twenty minutes. I talk to each customer, take notes, and deliver the finished product by 5:00 P.M. the next day. My prices start at five dollars for words only and go up to twenty dollars for words and concept.

Bobby Dunn has appointed himself my sales force; he recruits customers who he thinks need my services and gives each one a talk about the need for secrecy. Bobby will not accept money from me as payment—he reminds me hourly that he is doing this for Jesus—but he is glad to be thanked in testimonies.

By the beginning of the second week of camp, our director, Reverend Stewart, and the camp counselors were openly rejoicing about the power of the Spirit at work, as reflected in the moving personal testimonies being given night after night. Bobby Dunn has been testifying every other night and smiling at me at breakfast every morning. Patsy Lewis has taught me how to set my hair on big rollers, and I let it dry while I sit up writing testimonies. I have a perfect pageboy, a white Bible bulging with five-dollar bills, and I am popular. There are times when I forget my father.

On this last night of camp I am still at large. But although I have not been caught, I have decided I am not cut out to be a small business. There is the question of good help, for one thing. Bobby Dunn is no good for detail work—clearly, the less he knows about how my mind works, the better—and so I have turned to Missy Tucker. Missy loves Jesus and her father and disapproves of everything about me. I love her because she truly believes I can be saved and, until that happens, is willing to get into almost any trouble I can think of, provided I do not try to stop her from quoting the appropriate Scripture. Even so, she resisted being drawn into the testimony business for more than a week, giving in only after I sank low enough to introduce her to Bobby Dunn and point out that she would be able to apply her cut to the high cost of braces.

The truth is, the business needs Missy. I am no better a disciple of the Palmer Handwriting Method than I am of Christ or of my mother's standards of behavior. No one can read my writing. Missy has won the penmanship medal at E. M. Morrow Elementary School so many times there is talk that it will be retired when we go off to junior high in the fall. When she's done writing, my testimonies look like poems.

The value of Missy's cursive writing skills, however, is offset by the ways in which she manifests herself as a True Believer. I can tolerate the Scripture quoting, but her fears are something else. I am afraid of snakes and of not being asked to pledge my mother's sorority at Baylor, both standard fears in Cabin A. Missy is terrified of Eastern religions.

Her father, a religion professor at a small Baptist college, has two passions: world religions and big-game hunting. In our neighborhood, where not rotating the tires on the family Ford on a schedule is considered eccentric, Dr. Tucker wears a safari jacket to class and greets everyone the same way: "Hi, wallaby." Missy is not allowed to be afraid of the dead animals in her father's den, but a pronounced sensitivity to Oriental mysticism is thought to be acceptable in a young girl.

Unless I watch her, Missy cannot be trusted to resist inserting a paragraph into every testimony in which the speaker thanks the Lord Jesus for not having allowed him or her to be born a Buddhist. I tell Missy repeatedly that if every member of the camp baseball team suddenly begins to compare and contrast Zen and the tenets of Southern Baptist fundamentalism in his three-minute testimony, someone—even in this trusting place—is going to start to wonder.

She says she sees my point but keeps arguing for more "spiritual" content in the testimonies, a position in which she is enthusiastically supported by Bobby Dunn. Missy and Bobby have fallen in love; Bobby asked her to wear his friendship ring two nights ago, using his own words. What is art to me is faith—and now love—to Missy, and we are not as close as we were three weeks ago.

I am a success, but a lonely one, since there is no one I can talk to about either my success or my feelings. My brother, David, who normally can be counted on to protect me from myself and others, has only vague, Christian concern for me these days. He has fallen in love with Denise Meeker, universally regarded as the most spiritually developed girl in camp history, and he is talking about following my father into the ministry. I believe that when Denise goes home to Corpus Christi, David will remember law school, but in the meantime he is no comfort to me.

Now, from my place in the front row of the choir, I know that I will not have to worry about a going-out-of-business sale. What I have secretly wished for all summer is about to happen. I am going to get caught.

Ten minutes ago, during Reverend Stewart's introduction of visitors from the pulpit, I looked out at the crowd in the tent and saw my father walking down the center aisle. As I watched, he stopped every few rows to shake hands and say hello, as casual and full of good humor as if this were his church on a Sunday morning. He is a handsome man, and when he stopped at the pew near the front where David is sitting, I was struck by how much my father and brother look alike, their dark heads together as they smiled and hugged. I think of David as belonging to me, not to my father, but there was an unmistakable sameness in their movements that caught me by surprise, and my eyes filled with tears. Suddenly David pointed toward the choir, at me, and my father nodded his head and continued walking toward the front of the tent. I knew he had seen me, and I concentrated on looking straight ahead as he mounted the stairs to the stage and took a seat to the left of the altar. Reverend Stewart introduced him as the special guest preacher for the last night of camp, and for an instant I let myself believe that was the only reason he had come. He would preach and we would go home together tomorrow. Everything would be all right.

I hear a choked-off sound from my left and know without turning to look that it is Missy, about to cry. She has seen my father, too, and I touch her hand to remind her that no one will believe she was at fault. Because of me, teachers have been patiently writing "easily led" and "cries often" on Missy's report cards for years, and she is still considered a good girl. She won't get braces this year, I think, but she will be all right.

In the next moment two things happen at once. Missy starts to cry, really cry, and my father turns in his seat, looks at me, and then away. It is then that I realize that Missy has decided, without telling me, that straight teeth are not worth eternal damnation. She and Bobby Dunn have confessed, and my father has been called. Now, as he sits with his Bible in his hands and his head bowed, his profile shows none of the cheer of a moment before, and none of the successful-Baptist-preacher expressions I can identify. He does not look spiritual or joyful or weighted down by the burden of God's expectations. He looks furious.

There are more announcements than I ever remember hearing on the last night of camp: prayer lists, final volleyball standings, bus departure times, a Lottie Moon Stewardship Award for Denise Meeker. After each item, I forget I have no reason to expect Jesus to help me and I pray for one more; I know that as soon as the last announcement is read, Reverend Stewart will call for a time of personal testimonies before my father's sermon.

Even with my head down I can see Bobby Dunn sinking lower into a center pew and, next to him, Tim Bailey leaning forward, wanting to be first at the microphone. Tim is another of the Bishop School jocks, and he has combed his hair and put on Sunday clothes. In his left hand he is holding my master-work, reproduced on three-by-five cards. He paid me twenty-five dollars for it—the most I have ever charged—and it is the best piece of my career. The script calls for Tim to talk movingly about meeting God in a car-truck accident near Galveston, when he was ten. In a dramatic touch of which I am especially proud, he seems to imply that God was driving the truck.

Tim, I know, is doing this to impress a Baptist Academy girl who has told him she will go to her cotillion alone before she goes with a boy who doesn't know Jesus as his personal Lord and Savior. He is gripping the notecards as if they were Didi Thornton, and for the first time in a lifetime full of Bible verses, I see an application to my daily living. I truly am about to reap what I have sown.

The announcements end, and Reverend Stewart calls for testimonies. As Tim Bailey rises, so does my father. As he straightens up, he turns again to look at me, and this time he makes a gesture toward the pulpit. It is a mock-gallant motion, the kind I have seen him make to let my mother go first at miniature golf. For an instant that simple reminder that I am not an evil mutant—I have a family that plays miniature golf—makes me think again that everything will be all right. Then I realize what my father is telling me. Tim Bailey will never get to the pulpit to give my testimony. My father will get there first, will tell the worshipers in the packed tent his sorrow and regret over the misdeeds of his little girl. *His little girl.* He is going to do what I have never imagined in all my fantasies about this moment. He is going to forgive me.

Without knowing exactly how it has happened, I am standing up, half running from the choir seats to the pulpit. I get there first, before either my father or Tim, and before Reverend Stewart can even say my name, I give my personal testimony.

I begin by admitting what I have been doing for the past three weeks. I talk about being gripped by hate, unable to appreciate the love of my wonderful parents or of Jesus. I talk about making money from other campers who, in their honest desire to honor the Lord, became trapped in my web of wrongdoing.

Bobby Dunn is crying. To his left I can see Mr. Talliferro; something in his face, intent and unsmiling, makes me relax: I am a Draw. Everyone is with me now. I can hear Missy behind me, still sobbing into her hymnal, and to prove I can make it work, I talk about realizing how blessed I am to have been born within easy reach of God's healing love. I could have been born a Buddhist, I say, and the gratifying gasps from the audience make me certain I can say anything I want now.

For an instant I lose control and begin quoting poetry instead of Scripture. There is a shaky moment when all I can remember is bits of "Stopping by Woods on a Snowy Evening," but I manage to tie the verses back to a point about Christian choices. The puzzled looks on some faces give way to shouts of "Amen!" and as I look out at the rows of people in the green-and-white-striped tent I know I have won. I have written the best testimony anyone at camp has ever given.

I feel, rather than see, my father come to stand beside me, but I do not stop. As I have heard him do hundreds of times, I ask the choir to sing an invitational hymn and begin singing with them, "Softly and tenderly, Jesus is calling, calling to you and to me. Come home, come home. Ye who are weary, come home."

My father never does give a sermon.

While the hymn is still being sung, Bobby Dunn moves from his pew to the stage, and others follow. They hug me; they say they understand; they say they forgive me. As each one moves on to my father, I can hear him thanking them for their concern and saying, yes, he knows they will be praying for the family.

By ten o'clock, the last knot of worshipers has left the tent, and my father and I are alone on the stage. He is looking at me without speaking; there is no expression on his face that I have seen before. "Daddy," I surprise myself by saying. Daddy is a baby name that I have not used since my ninth birthday. My father raises his left hand and slaps me, hard, on my right cheek. He catches me as I start to fall, and we sit down together on the steps leading from the altar. He uses his handkerchief to clean blood from underneath my eye, where his Baylor ring has opened the skin. As he works the white square of cloth carefully around my face, I hear a sound I have never heard before, and I realize my father is crying. I am crying, too, and the mixture of tears and blood on my face makes it impossible to see him clearly. I reach for him anyway and am only a little surprised when he is there.

BRYAN WOOLLEY

Burgers, Beer, and
Patsy Cline

I love a good joint. By "joint" I mean a drinking—and eating—establishment where, whatever else is for sale, the main merchandise is beer. And where the bartender is the owner or his son or a guy who has worked there so long that it's impossible to imagine the place without him. And the waitress calls all customers of both sexes either "Hon" or "Darlin'." Pool and shuffleboard are desirable options, but not essential. *Absolutely* essential, however, is a good jukebox loaded with genuine country music.

Adair's is such a place.

One neon sign in front says it's Adair's Saloon. Another says it's Adair's Bar & Grill. The T-shirt on the waitress says it's Adair's Beer Joint. The regulars just call it Adair's, and if you're a Dallas-dweller of a certain type, Adair's is heaven.

Looking at some of the customers at lunchtime, you know what has happened. These guys have walked out of some glass office tower, out of some meeting with a boss or a banker, the heat on the street has hit them like a ton of lighted charcoal, their suit coats have begun to fit like straitjackets, and they can't stand the thought of one more person telling them to have a nice day.

And somebody has said, "Hey, this is an Adair's kind of day!" And they've crawled into a car and driven over to that long, narrow, shady room at 2624 Commerce Street in Deep Ellum. They've probably told themselves that they're going to have a quick burger and get back to the office, but they've probably lied.

Ordering lunch is easy at Adair's. You get a hamburger, or you get a cheeseburger. Lettuce, tomato, pickle, and onion. Choice of mustard, catsup, or mayonnaise. The bread is a hamburger bun just like the ones your mother used to buy at the grocery store. The meat is gray and greasy and weighs half a pound. The cheese on the cheeseburger is American. The whole thing is topped with a jalapeno and held together with a toothpick and served in a plastic basket.

It's the kind of burger you used to buy a long time ago in places called Joe's and Louie's and Pancho's, where the burgers were built by Joe or Louie or Pancho in person. Joe's or Louie's or Pancho's might have offered you a few alternatives—ham-and-cheese, say, or egg salad—but Adair's doesn't. If you don't want a burger, you don't eat at Adair's.

On the side, you can get plain potato chips or barbecue potato chips or potato chips with those little grooves in them or Fritos. The side dishes cost extra and come in sacks. To drink, there are your basic American soft drinks and your basic American beers, served with the cans still on them. You can get a drink of the hard stuff, too, if you don't order anything fancy.

For those who liked Joe's or Louie's or Pancho's, Adair's provides the best lunch available in the vicinity of downtown

Dallas. But the best thing about Adair's isn't the lunch. It's the place you get to eat it in.

If you grew up in Fort Stockton or Round Rock or Durant or Odessa or some other place that had a real beer joint and you sometimes get homesick, entering Adair's will bring a tear to your eye. The long room is dark and cool, lighted only by the sun through the front plate-glass window and the half-dozen neon beer signs on the walls and cooled by a big air conditioner that hangs from the ceiling and by ceiling fans.

Also on the ceiling are hundreds of gimme caps that somebody nailed up there and hundreds of paper napkins that customers have wadded up, soaked in beer, and thrown up there to stick during the bar's two and one-half years on Commerce Street, where it moved after twenty years on Cedar Springs Road.

The walls, adorned with Texas, Confederate, and American flags and portraits of Bob Wills, John Wayne, and Hondo Crouch, also are full of words. Some are rules and information posted by Adair's management:

You Daince With Who Brung You Or No Damn Daincing.

Dress Code Enforced: Clean Clothes.

Yes! We Serve Crabs. Have A Seat.

Bob Wills Lives.

Public Notice: As A Public Service Announcement,
This Establishment Will Notify The Next Of Kin
Of Any Person Who Dares Drop A Puck
On This Damn New Table.

This reference is to the shuffleboard table, which stands along the wall between the two pool tables at the front of the room and the pinball machines farther back, near the patched, vinyl-covered booths and wobbly tables.

There are other signs that used to stand beside Texas highways, identifying or directing motorists to Hondo Creek, Tarpley, Bandera, Orangefield, and, of course, Camp Adair. But most of the words on the walls were written by customers.

The Adair's graffiti collection must be the largest in Dallas, and it covers the entire spectrum of the graffitist's art: classic restroom poetry, insults of all known ethnic groups, praise and abuse of various universities and fraternities, individual brags and lies signed with names or initials, comments on Texas foreign policy (*The Border Patrol is on the wrong river*), and bits of personal philosophy (*As I look back the only thing I would of saved for my old age is the years between twenty and thirty*). Some very tall customers, including the Secret Service agents who guarded Vice President George Bush during the Republican National Convention in 1984, wrote their remarks on the ceiling.

But the soul of Adair's, the thing that makes Adair's *Adair's,* is the music. "We have some who come in for lunch and stay all afternoon listening to the jukebox," says Charline Johnston, who hefts the burgers from the cook's window to the tables.

The Adair's jukebox is simply the best country jukebox in Dallas, probably the best in Texas. So in the very shadows of downtown's towers, within earshot of Central Expressway's roar, the good old grown-up country boys take off their suit coats, loosen their neckties, nurse a cool one and sing along with Hank Williams on "Cold, Cold Heart," Hank Thompson on "The Wild Side of Life," Bob Wills on "Faded Love," Webb Pierce on "There Stands the Glass," Patsy Cline on "I Fall to Pieces," Ernest Tubb on "Walking the Floor Over You." Some even try to imitate Jimmie Rodgers' blue yodel on "Muleskinner Blues," accompanied by the click of pool balls, the ping of pinball, and many fractures of the *No Profanity* rule.

Eyes glaze and minds slide easily into memories of two-stepping thigh to thigh with some long-ago sweetie in some faraway high school gym, of sweaty adolescent grapplings in the backseats of '53 Fords under the bright Southwestern moon, of the first beer drunk—illegally, probably—in a joint much like this.

In Adair's, on such a hot afternoon, it's hard to remember you're really a lawyer or a judge or a cop or a computer programmer or a truck driver or an auto parts salesman who still has work to do. It's even harder to care.

LAWRENCE WRIGHT

Escape

I left Dallas on the afternoon train, bound for Tulane University in the city most unlike Dallas that I knew of: New Orleans. My hair was cut short and I wore a black suit. I had the idea from reading magazines that college students were carefully dressed nearly all the time.

There was a feeling I had whenever I traveled from Texas to Louisiana that I was moving back in time. Trains throw you off time anyway, since you are always passing the rear of things—people's backyards, the back ends of buildings, nothing ever faces onto the tracks—and the rear of things is timeless. Louisiana has a starkly uncharming antebellum quality about the tarpaper shacks in the countryside and the skinny black children waving at the train that never stops for them. It is the South, the Deep South, which doesn't begin, as far as Texans are concerned, until you cross the Sabine River. There is an air of prehistory about this country of mossy trees and dark water. From the train window it would be easy to imagine the Louisiana landscape as a Disneyland cyclorama in which some gigantic mechanical sauropod would lurch out of the swamp and we would all scream.

Outside of Berkeley, American campuses were very much under control in 1965. For the freshman on the train, the word "collegiate" was still a fashion statement. I had never heard anyone speak of "relevance" concerning my studies, or "imperialism" in connection with my own country. "Oppression" and "Third World" were ideas so freshly coined that I hadn't tested their worth. The events that were going to change my life and my country had already been set in motion, however. Watts had burned. Operation Rolling Thunder—the bombing of North Vietnam—was under way. Betty Friedan had published *The Feminine Mystique* two years earlier, although as yet there were very few women aware of feminism as a movement. The Pill had made its debut in 1960, and it was beginning to find its way into the hands of unmarried coeds, most of whom, in my experience, obtained prescriptions through dermatologists who were willing to support the conceit that it cleared up acne. The student revolt, prompted by the war, had not yet been announced, although something momentous was bound to happen, given the extraordinary numbers of students entering the nation's universities. I had never heard of Haight-Ashbury. I had never smelled the sweet, acrid odor of marijuana. The Gulf of Tonkin was a headline, but I seldom read the news. Why should I? Wasn't college a sanctuary where the gates closed on daily life? I should turn my attention now to the eternal, not the ephemeral, to Latin grammar and the Wife of Bath and the complexities of cell division, not Western movies and baseball box scores and news of the world.

I shared a cabinette on the train with another Tulane freshman named John Scurry, who was going to study architecture. I envied him his resolution. I was still trying on professions, hoping to discover myself among the infinite possibilities. I wanted to be a writer, but in my mind writers were a chosen race, like the Jews, with whom they frequently coincided. Over the summer I had endured a battery of aptitude tests, with inconclusive results. "Just don't go into medicine," the counselor advised me. I showed no talent for it and, until then, no interest. But the thought of losing an option was unbearable. Immediately after the test I contacted a family friend who was a doctor and began making rounds with him. He took me on a tour of his charity cancer patients, condemned men and women in shuttered rooms, and although I knew from the first glance of their incurious eyes that I would never make a doctor, I held on to the option. I told my cabin mate that I was going to study pre-med.

Hurricane Betsy struck us in Alexandria, Louisiana. By the time she reached us she had already devastated New Orleans and flooded the lower Mississippi valley. The train came to a dead stop on a blank stretch of track fifteen miles beyond the city and sat there, all systems shut down, for eighteen hours. At first it was thrilling—the thrashing winds, the incredible pounding rain—but there was too much security on the train even in the face of a hurricane to believe in danger, so we began to think of other things, such as the absence of air-conditioning, the loss of the dining car in Alexandria, the odor of the other passengers. At first we were all in it together. Gradually we fell into cliques. We began snapping at each other; it was easy to see cannibalism lurking ahead. A honeymooning couple grew alarmed after ten hours of this and decided to flee the train. I recall them disappearing into the sheets of the storm, carrying their suitcases back up the track toward civilization.

When we arrived in New Orleans it was as if the Bomb had fallen. Oak trees were ripped up by their roots; automobiles had been tossed about like toys. The cabbie who picked me up at the station was in a state of exhilaration. He pointed out the ironic symbols of destruction. We passed a Conoco station with all the consonants blown off the sign, and a Shell station with no S. The health department was in a panic, the cabbie told me excitedly, because Betsy had washed the cadavers out of the raised cemetery vaults, and old bodies mingled in the flood with the freshly dead. On the streets I noticed people picking their way through shards of glass and broken tree limbs, staring at each other with dazzled smiles.

New Orleans was old and rotten, corrupt, depraved, licentious, a grand old whore who had enjoyed herself too much but was still generous enough to give pleasure to someone else, someone new. It was a Catholic town and indifferent to progress. After the charmlessness of Dallas I fell in love with the overripe splendor of New Orleans: the great homes of the Garden District, with their huge trees and ivied yards, and the long verandahs where the plutocrats sat in rocking chairs and drank gin fizzes; the rows of pastel shotgun cottages (ordered out of the Sears catalog), which filled the Irish Channel district and ran down Magazine Street in front of the wharves; the glorious depravity of the French Quarter, deeply anchored in history— but a history of pirates and voodoo and jazz. I walked the streets of New Orleans in a state of aesthetic liberation, every bit as much of an émigré as Hemingway in Paris, and feeling at one with him and with all the great American writers. For hadn't they all stopped in New Orleans on their way to immortality—Whitman, Twain, Faulkner, Anderson, Williams, Capote—and which of them had ever passed a night in Dallas?

I was impressed right away that they sold beer in the five-and-dime and French wine in drugstores. Also, that I could buy it, a legal right I exercised with enthusiasm. In Dallas, when we teenagers wanted a drink, we would loiter outside a liquor store until we spotted some old black man in the parking lot. We'd give him five dollars for a case of beer and let him keep the change. In New Orleans liquor of all sorts was freely available and only marginally more expensive than tap water. A mixed drink at Larry & Katz's, which was a half-finished shack where the clientele sat on upturned liquor boxes and the bartenders wore revolvers, cost twenty-five cents. It was a fine place to start the evening.

From there a person might wander over to Felix's for oysters. In the too-bright fluorescent light, the oysters looked like puddles of mercury. Here in Felix's you could see the classes converge, however briefly. There were handsomely barbered men and women in evening clothes, truck drivers in poplin uniforms with their names embroidered above their breast pockets, Tulane literature professors in tweed jackets with elbow patches, lawyers and criminals, doctors and patients, professional bowlers—all of them engaged in the singularly barbaric act of eating living animals by the dozen. You could close your eyes and place a person in his class by the sound of his language. The rich Orleanian has a slowed-down, muffled tone like a record played at three-quarter speed; I have heard the word "mayonnaise" delivered with so much nuance that it occupied the space of a sentence and arrived with its own internal marks of punctuation, rather like "My, uh . . . *Nay!* uzzz?" The most characteristic speech of the city is an urban dialect otherwise associated with Brooklyn and Hoboken, a "dems" and "dose" kind of talk that originated with the Irish laborers who were brought in to build the levees. When city people greeted each other they'd cry "Where y'at, ya muddah?" so college kids referred to townies as "where-y'ats" or just "yats."

I became a food romantic. In 1965 New Orleans was one of the few American cities that took food seriously. Now, when there is scarcely a middle-sized town in the country without a representative sampling of international cuisine, as well as health food stores, specialty gourmet shops, fresh pasta, excellent bakeries, wonderful coffee, it is hard to remember how boring and desolate the American diet was. The only cookbooks on my mother's shelf were Miz Rombauer's *The Joy of Cooking* and Fannie Farmer's *The Boston Cooking School Cookbook*—both of them wedding gifts received by nearly every war bride in America. I grew up on meat loaf and mashed potatoes. When I was a child in Abilene, Texas, in the fifties, we would drive out to the local Air Force base after church to eat Sunday dinner—it was practically the only decent kitchen in West Texas. One of the great days of my childhood was when the first franchised restaurant came into my life: It was Kentucky Fried Chicken, and it caused a sensation. Now this was cooking! We went there every week and felt grateful, positively blessed, that Colonel Sanders would grant a concession to such a podunk town as Abilene. Even in Dallas in the sixties, Italian and Chinese restaurants were novelties. Pizza parlors were just catching on. The only exotic restaurant was La Tunisia, and its principal attraction was the seven-foot Negro who opened the door.

I spent part of my college career as a busboy and then as a waiter in one of the handsome small restaurants in the Quarter. My promotion was due entirely to my being the only busboy who owned a tuxedo. It gave me incredible pleasure to present the menus and watch the flushed, candlelit faces puzzle over the snapper versus the veal, taking those little internal soundings ("Do I feel like crabmeat tonight?"). I learned my way around the alleyways and kitchen doors that led to the secret chambers of Brennan's or Antoine's, where I might be dispatched to borrow a gallon of remoulade sauce. In the kitchens of those great restaurants were corpulent black men assembling dishes out of great troughs of condiments. I would dash back down the alley with the remoulade, up the rear stairs, into the kitchen, where I would pick up my entrées and walk slowly, with a sense of composure and purpose, into the dining room.

I had a hunger for bohemia. I wanted to see life raw and unpredictable. Later I recognized this as the Private School Syndrome—this idealization of the hard life, this romancing of the proletariat—but then it was all new and entirely original. I began to haunt the waterfront bars: the Acropolis, the Seven Seas, and particularly La Casa de los Marinos, a wonderful dive in the Quarter across from the Toulouse Street wharf, where sailors came to dance to Latin music and pick up college girls. French sailors were usually the most successful in this pursuit, owing to their tasseled berets, which were prized by the undergraduates of Sophie Newcomb College. For the most part, however, the students and the sailors didn't mix; they crowded together in an uneasy emulsion of culture, language, and class.

Until I came to New Orleans I had never met an acknowledged homosexual. In Dallas we had spoken of queers, but no one I knew had ever spotted one—they were like Communists, an unseen menace. I was always hearing about the practice of "rolling queers" in Lee Park; in fact, I had the idea that homosexuals existed (if at all) only to sit on park benches and wait to be mugged by indignant teenaged boys. In New Orleans, however, there was an active, aboveground homosexual culture (the word "gay" had not yet been bent to this purpose), which was wildly dramatic and self-consciously humorous. The center of the scene was deep in the Quarter at a bar called Dixie's. During Mardi Gras I would go there, safely ensconced in a phalanx of fraternity brothers, to watch the transvestite beauty contest at the corner of Bourbon and St. Ann. Some of the contestants were disconcertingly beautiful, despite the telltale Adam's apples and powdered whiskers. One year a contingent of Marines from the USS *Forrestal* came swaggering past. They were all drinking Hurricanes—those giant tumblers of liquor from Pat O'Brien's that usually signaled the drunken tourist. A moment later the Marines were on the stage with the contestants, hugging, kissing, groping, and quickly being hustled off into cabs. I wonder what they had to say to each other on the *Forrestal* the next morning.

It never occurred to me not to join a fraternity. Being a student was not yet the serious business it would become, and besides, I had an affinity for mystic societies and secret handshakes. By the time I graduated, fraternities had become passé, a redoubt for social reactionaries, but in 1965 we still believed, with

217

Barry Goldwater, that "wherever fraternities are not allowed, Communism flourishes." My lodge, Delta Tau Delta, was housed in two condemned buildings on Broadway, with no air-conditioning and with a plumbing system that backed up under the foundations. Our housemother was a fat, elderly woman who walked around with a dachshund tucked under her arm. She was as ribald as any of the brothers, but she always dressed for dinner, and we were supposed to mind our manners around her. One of the conceits of fraternity life, despite all evidence, is that it gives a man polish. I had to remind myself, when I was stepping over unconscious upperclassmen in order to throw up in the community toilet, that I was gaining advantages.

Your fraternity was supposed to say something about the kind of person you were. Indeed, there seemed to be an intuitive truth about this association of man and lodge that was not bound to a single campus. It was like a horoscope in that respect. The SAEs were campus leaders, politicians, snobs who spent their spare time buying golf sweaters. The Dekes were good-natured drunks. The Sigma Chis were serious, dull, marginal nerds. The KAs were unreconstructed Confederates. Once they planted cotton in their front yard and sent their black porter out with a gunnysack to pick it. During homecoming one year, when our football team was playing the University of Alabama, the KAs built a two-story papier-mâché Kotex box in front of their house, with the legend STOP THE CRIMSON TIDE. The Delts were known, universally and accurately, as party boys.

The biggest party of all was Mardi Gras. The carnival season lasted from Twelfth Night (January 6) until Fat Tuesday, the night before Ash Wednesday. In that space of time, which was sometimes as long as two months, depending on the date of Easter, the city rollicked in one long bacchanal. New Orleans society divided itself into krewes—Comus, Rex, Momus, and Proteus were the big ones, and the Zulus for the blacks—and they put on spectacular parades. First came the flambeaux dancers, black teenagers twirling flaming batons, doing a shuffle-step dance to the music of the brass band that followed; then came the floats sailing through the Quarter like galleons. On the last day of carnival the streets filled with a million drunks in makeup and costumes, searching for sin on the eve of the season of repentance.

One of my fraternity brothers, Arthur Wright, who was also from Dallas (but no relation of mine), rented an apartment on Royal Street for carnival. It was a cheap efficiency in an old Creole house with a single large bed and a bricked-up fireplace. Arthur and I came to furnish it one night before the big parades began, and we were surprised to find someone else living there. As a matter of fact, Arthur learned, the apartment had been rented to three different people during the past week. He received this information from the landlord in an angry phone call. The landlord said he'd be right over.

He screeched up to the curb on a motorcycle, with his wife sitting in a sidecar. She wore a white plastic overcoat and a turquoise hairnet. Her husband was a paunchy little Cajun with a leather jacket and curly black hair. "I ain't gon' 'pologize," he told Arthur, "'cause I got you one far better dan dis on Bourbon Street. You gon lak it fine."

We followed the landlord's motorcycle down to lower Bourbon, well past the tourist zone into a darkened stretch of tenements. For two Dallas boys it was a little darker and more menacing than we were prepared for. I noticed right away, when we came into the courtyard, that there were no windows or doors on the apartments, just gauzy curtains and beaded portieres, through which we could see fleshy women and men in undershirts smoking cigarettes. In a pale orange room a naked man was playing the saxophone.

Now this is the demimonde, I was thinking to myself, as an adolescent Mexican girl came down the stairs wearing a sarong. "My mistress," the landlord acknowledged. "Rita, bring me my blades."

She nodded and went into a room, returning with a carved wooden box. Inside, encased in green felt, were a dozen throwing knives. The landlord's wife stood against a wall fifteen feet away, with her arms spread in the crucifix position.

Whoomp! The first blade struck in the niche below her armpit. The mistress handed the landlord another knife and stood back to watch. Her mouth was partly open, and her tongue moved slowly across the edge of her upper incisors.

"I'm having second thoughts about this apartment," I whispered to Arthur.

Whoomp! Other armpit.

"They certainly have a trusting relationship," Arthur observed.

Whoomp, whoomp, whoomp! The wife stared unblinkingly as the knives tumbled toward her. Her husband finished with a nice flourish, placing the last blade an inch above her forehead. Arthur and I watched with maniac grins.

As the wife came away, leaving her outline pinned against the wall, I happened to see through her turquoise hair net. Half an ear was missing.

At last—real life!

There was a brief time in my life when my parents and I agreed on the music; it was the middle fifties, when Gisele MacKienzie and Dorothy Collins sang the popular songs on "Your Hit Parade." Snooky Lanson sang "Davy Crockett" week after week, and I knew every verse. At night, when I was supposed to be asleep, I would tune into WWL from New Orleans and listen to the smart sounds of the big bands playing the Blue Room of the Roosevelt Hotel. Then Elvis Presley sang "Hound Dog," and I began to give way to the tidal pull of rock and roll.

There was in my mind a certain suspicion that the music of my time would never be as sophisticated as that of my parents. Perhaps it was because their generation regarded rock and roll with contempt and bewilderment that the music became defiant. I remember being absolutely thrilled by the rumor that Gene Vincent had said "fuckin'" in "Woman Love"—although what he actually said was unintelligible. That the churches and the politicians were scandalized gave the music a political importance it had never aspired to have. I identified with the music, but I held back, too; it wasn't all I wanted it to be. Even when the Beatles came to America in February 1964, singing "I Want to Hold Your Hand" and "She Loves You," I didn't surrender to them. They were okay, I thought, but I didn't understand why the girls were screaming and the boys were suddenly growing their hair long.

The music hit me in 1966. I was walking into the University Center as Simon and Garfunkel were singing "Sounds of Silence" on the jukebox. The ambience was specific to me. The Mamas and the Papas sang "Monday, Monday." It was the year when everything I heard seemed to be drawn from some generational oversoul, and I resonated without thinking or resisting. I had the feeling of being in a movie and every song I heard was part of my own soundtrack. It was a year when soul music broke through, at least for me. Percy Sledge sang "When a Man Loves a Woman" and Ray Charles sang "Cryin' Time." I had just discovered the great soul singers of New Orleans, Irma Thomas and Benny Spellman. How odd it seems, when I reflect on the music of 1966, that the number one song that year was "The Ballad of the Green Berets."

In the fall of 1967 my roommate, Allan Denchfield, rigged his record player to a timer, so that every morning of the semester we awakened to the Beatles' *Sgt. Pepper* album. We couldn't get enough of it. We listened to Leonard Cohen singing "Suzanne." In the spring of 1968 the radio never stopped playing Otis Redding singing "(Sittin' on) The Dock of the Bay." Otis was already dead when that record came out, which seemed eerie then, although we soon got used to death being a feature of the music. I was eating crawfish in Eddie Price's bar the first time I heard Janis Joplin growl the opening of "Turtle Blues," and after that I always listened for the spot where her bottle of Southern Comfort shattered on the beat. Her sound was raw, insinuating, and powerfully ambiguous— neither black nor white, male nor female, but some revolutionary middle note between the races and the sexes. She was, it seemed to me, the Siren of our generation, beckoning us to the dangerous margins where death awaited.

The great object of college was not learning but sex. The sexual revolution may have been under way, but it was still unnamed and unacknowledged, and like all revolutions it started far away, on the sophisticated seacoasts, not in the Deep South. Here, one could only just now feel the moorings loosening on the Victorian Age. The girls of Newcomb College, Tulane's sister school, were highly proper ladies. They were also as closely guarded as convicts after ten o'clock on weeknights.

There is something feral about the needs of young men, something well outside the boundaries of civilized behavior. We had all heard about the sophomore geologist so cramped from desire ("blue balls" it was called) that it required three men to carry him to the infirmary. Many nights I would stand outside the women's dorm and find myself close to baying. Once, when I was standing there with a fraternity brother, and we had just returned our dates to the custody of their rooms, we decided to break into the dorm. I stood on my friend's shoulders and was just able to knock on my date's window, which she opened, quite obligingly. I crawled in and reached down for my friend, but as I was hauling him up a security patrolman grabbed his ankle. There was an awkward tug-of-war, which I lost. Then I heard the alarms.

It is a stupid feeling to be fleeing down a corridor to the screams of coeds, searching for an exit. All the doors were chained. I heard a commotion behind me, which I took to be the security patrol. I dove into a stairwell and nearly trompled a girl in curlers and a nightgown, whose mouth made a little *o* as I went flying past. I was in the basement, trapped, I realized, in the darkened laundry room.

How was I to know, as my pulse beat out a drumroll between the washers and dryers, that I was the last victim of the Age of Innocence? Liberation was riding to the rescue, but it would not reach me in time. I would be captured and returned to Dallas in disgrace (me, the once-promising student, led astray by boiling hormones). Or else—jail! Breaking and entering! My life in tatters! I heard the boots clumping down the stairs. I edged back into the shadows, and felt—a door. I hit it with everything I had. As I burst outside and fled through the shrubbery, I heard the sound of women cheering.

There was a constant search for private places. The college acted, in the phrase of the day, in loco parentis, and consequently unlocked empty spaces were rarely found and highly valued. Practically the only such places were the practice rooms in the music building; I spent several dates hugging and kissing under the legs of a studio piano. Sometimes, I discovered, the very most public places had privacy hidden inside them—the Newcomb auditorium, for instance, which was usually dark, lent an interesting theatrical setting to my frustrated sexual pursuits. Once, when the auditorium was locked, my girlfriend and I were drifting around campus and came upon Tulane's famous stadium, where the Sugar Bowl is played. The fence was thirteen feet high, but we scaled it and wandered into the vast black space. There was a murmurous, echoing sound like a seashell held against the ear. Small slivers of light reflected around the elliptical tiers, ring after expanding ring. We felt ourselves to be in the center of the universe, we were all that existed, we were life itself. It is a memory that is recaptured for me every New Year's Day when I watch the Sugar Bowl game and see the fifty-yard line, where I finally scored.

At Tulane we began to hear about the student movement against the war, but we were buried in the Confederacy, and the idea of protest seemed foreign and rather crackpot. None-theless, it happened that the first mass student protest in the South took place one midnight at Tulane in 1968, when 350 students marched on President Longenecker's home to protest the censorship of two "pornographic" photographs in the school literary journal (one of the pictures was of a naked art instructor). We had no idea what to expect, or even how to go about staging a protest. A graduate student, a woman who had gone to Berkeley, stood up and told us what to do when the police came. "Link arms, then lie down like you're dead," she said. Of course, the police never came; in fact, no one noticed us at all.

That march was a small act of repentance on my part. The year before, I had encountered the first demonstration I had ever seen: a group of about fifteen students protesting the de-cision to hold the homecoming dance on board the *President,* the paddle-wheel steamboat that ported conventioneers up and down the Mississippi to the sound of white Dixieland jazz. It was a segregated boat. The management was making an excep-tion to accommodate the Tulane student body, which included a very small number of blacks, and Dionne Warwick, who was going to perform. That seemed like progress to me—hadn't we forced a change in policy? The protesters wanted another site for the dance. They were standing outside the University Cen-ter with signs saying DO NOT SUPPORT RACIST INSTITUTIONS and NO STUDENT MONEY FOR SEGREGATION. I was walking from class with a friend, and we both thought of the same hilarious idea. We would protest the protest. We made a couple of signs, BAN THE BOMB and PREPARE TO MEET THY GOD, then we sidled up to the demonstration and stood there, trying to keep straight faces.

Some fraternity brothers came by and applauded. My pic-ture was published in the student newspaper. There I am, with a smirk, in the last half of the sixties, on the cusp of the seismic changes that would characterize that era. All around the country protest was making itself heard, in the causes of peace, brotherhood, racial justice, but at that moment I thought it was something to ridicule.

The next week I went to pick up Dionne Warwick at the airport. I was the welcoming committee. I gave her a dozen roses and drove her downtown to one of the grand old hotels. She was the first black woman, other than my maid, that I had ever driven anywhere. She was charming and glamorous. I was completely enchanted. We talked about football. She followed the Philadelphia Eagles, who were playing the Dallas Cowboys that Sunday, and we made a twenty-dollar bet on the game.

When we got to the hotel there was a flurry at the desk. Suddenly they couldn't find her reservation. It took me more than a minute to realize that the hotel was segregated too. Not legally, of course—the Civil Rights Act of 1964 had been passed—but in that insolent, closed-face fashion that says we never have a vacancy for black people. The bellmen hadn't even bothered to pick up her luggage. Miss Warwick was standing there with her roses, and I saw for the first time that look—an ancient look of burned-out anger and humiliated pride. I suddenly felt sick about my idiocy of the week before. I had made fun of something I clearly hadn't understood. That was the force of the repression for which I, being white, was responsible. The manager of the hotel came to the desk to deliver the excuse, but I cut him off. "You are about to make a terrible mistake," I told him. "This is Dionne Warwick. Don't you know who she is?" He looked blank. "She's one of the most popular singers in the world. If you don't give her a room, and a really good one, you're going to be in every newspaper in the country tomorrow morning."

He suddenly discovered a room key.

This was my only triumph for right and decency in my four years of undergraduate life. I never paid Dionne Warwick her twenty dollars, however (the Cowboys lost on Sunday).

*　　*　　*

225

I had come to New Orleans to escape Dallas, but I had not left the assassination behind me. The madness followed. New Orleans was Oswald's city, his birthplace, and his spirit hung over the place like an evil spell. Soon New Orleans would be lit up in one of those queer American binges of lunacy, a paranoia of conspiracy that has been part of the national psyche since the Salem witch trials.

On Bourbon Street one day near the end of my freshman year I met Delilah, who would play a small but fatal part in the craziness to come. She was a stripper who did an Egyptian belly dance to "Hava Nagila," the Hebrew song of celebration. She was clearly not reading the latest news from the Middle East. I introduced myself as a representative of Tulane's Cosmopolitan Committee. One of the committee's purposes, I explained, was to bring interesting cultural acts—such as hers—to the university. I had the idea of billing her as a "Jewish-Egyptian ethnic dancer" and letting her take off her clothes in McAlister Auditorium.

Delilah agreed to meet me at the club the following Tuesday, and at the appointed time I appeared. There was a Grayline bus tour parked outside, and the place was filled with Iowa chiropractors who were nursing their four-dollar drinks and watching Lynda Bridgette, the World's Largest Stripper, shake her 378 pounds as the stage creaked and moaned.

"Delilah's expecting me," I told the barmaid in my best Peter Gunn style (I was eighteen years old).

"Oh sure."

"No, really."

She gave me a look that said this better be real, and went back to the dressing room. I took a seat. In a moment Delilah came out and shimmied through her big number. She had a shiny appendectomy scar that I hadn't noticed before, but in the stage lights it seemed phosphorescent. Then, to the admiring astonishment of the Iowans, Delilah came to my table and ordered a Dr Pepper. She was in her mid-thirties, I calculated, or a little older—twice my age, in any case. She had black hair and olive-toned skin, which was probably the inspiration for casting herself as an Egyptian. However, she affected a Zsa Zsa Gabor accent along the lines of "Vere are you from, dahlink?" She was a walking cultural malaprop.

I admitted I was from Dallas.

"No kidding? *Dallas?*"

Her Hungarian accent fell aside and was replaced by the more familiar nasal tones of North Texas. I asked if she knew Dallas. "Yeah," she said, "I know that goddamn town too well." We sat quietly for a moment. Being from Dallas was an awkward bond to share.

"I used to work for Jack Ruby," she volunteered.

She seemed to want to talk about him. He was a nice man, she remembered, but "a little crazy." It was Ruby, the Jewish impresario, who put her together with "Hava Nagila." Delilah gave me her telephone number, and I told her I would call next semester concerning her performance at Tulane. She said I could come to her apartment for "coffee."

All summer long I thought about that invitation.

I was already alarmed at the direction my life was taking. When I fled Dallas for the university, I left behind a sweet Christian girlfriend. She had given me a Bible for my eighteenth birthday. "Cherish this book always, Larry, and diligently read it," she admonished on the flyleaf, but I had fallen into the hands of the Sybarites and the existentialists, and when I returned to Dallas that summer I felt like a moral double agent. Half of me was sitting with my girlfriend in church, underlining Scripture with a yellow marker, and half (more than half) was scheming of ways to lead my little Christian exemplar into one of life's dark passageways.

I was lying on her lap, with that thought in mind, watching the ten o'clock news, when a photograph of a black-haired woman in a belly dancing costume flashed on the screen.

"That's Delilah!" I said, sitting up.

"*What?*"

"Shh. I know her."

Her name, it turned out, was Marilyn Magyar Walle. She had just been murdered in Omaha, shot eight times by a man she had been married to for a month. Her association with Jack Ruby was noted. My girlfriend looked at me with an expression of confounded decency.

"Do you have something you want to tell me, Larry?"

I wasn't the only one who marked Delilah's death. The conspiracists were keeping a list of "witnesses" who had died since the assassination, a list that grew and grew. By February 1967 seventeen others had died, including two more strippers who had worked for Ruby (one was shot to death, the other was found hanging by her toreador pants in a Dallas jail cell). Most of these deaths were from natural causes or explainable under other circumstances, but in the aggregate they had a weight they wouldn't have had by themselves. Seven of the victims had given testimony to the Warren Commission, six others had been interviewed by the Dallas police or the FBI. What are the chances, one might wonder, that so many people connected with the assassination would be dead in three and a half years? An actuary in London said the odds against all of them being dead in that time were 100,000 trillion to one—a figure that throws mysterious shadows across the otherwise unmysterious fates of car wrecks, failing hearts, jealous husbands, and disappointed suicides.

Like the majority of Americans, I wondered if the whole story had been told. Was there only one assassin on November 22, 1963? What about the Zapruder film, which seemed to show the President being shot from the front, not from Oswald's angle in the upper rear? Were there other assassins on the grassy knoll? Was Oswald framed? There were enough unexplained questions in my mind that I was prepared to believe the New Orleans district attorney, Jim Garrison, when he announced on March 1, 1967, that he had solved the case.

"Big Jim" Garrison was already a heroic presence in the

city. He was a reformer with a New Orleanian sense of ethical balance. He had cleaned up Bourbon Street, which meant keeping the G-strings on the dancers and getting rid of the streetwalkers. He cracked down on gambling operations in Orleans Parish but left intact the sacrosanct pinball machines, which paid off at the rate of a nickel a game (I had several friends who went to school on a "pinball scholarship"). The big gambling syndicates fled next door, to Jefferson Parish, out of Big Jim's grasp. Garrison had the reputation of a man who feared neither the moral zealots nor the local mob; he was tough, unbribable, cagey, unorthodox. Plus he had the power to issue subpoenas. He seemed to be the perfect man to solve the crime of the century.

What his investigation did, however, was to dip a ladle into the bizarre society of the New Orleans underworld, which was filled with mercenaries and mobsters, CIA agents, disaffected priests, and YMCA homosexuals. Somehow all of these creatures combined themselves in a single person, a man the district attorney called "one of history's most important individuals." Unfortunately, David W. Ferrie had already joined the list of the mysteriously dead.

Eastern Airlines had fired Ferrie as a pilot after he was arrested for a "crime against nature" with a sixteen-year-old boy. He had been a leader of the local Civil Air Patrol, which Lee Harvey Oswald joined in 1954. Robert Oswald suspected Ferrie of introducing his brother to Communism, but Ferrie's politics seem to have been oriented in another direction. He once wrote a letter to the secretary of defense asking for an opportunity to "train killers." "There is nothing I would enjoy better than blowing the hell out of every damn Russian, Communist, Red or what-have-you." He may have been given his chance when the CIA drilled anti-Castro Cubans in the backwaters of Lake Pontchartrain. Ferrie later claimed to have taken part in the Bay of Pigs invasion.

On the day of Kennedy's assassination, Ferrie was in a

courtroom with his boss, Carlos Marcello, the godfather of the New Orleans Mafia, a man who had his own good reasons for wanting the President dead. The president's brother, Attorney General Robert Kennedy, had deported Marcello to Guatemala. (According to legend, Guatemalan authorities transported him to El Salvador, where he was dropped into the jungle wearing a silk suit and alligator shoes.) Ferrie supposedly rescued Marcello from the tropics and smuggled him back to the United States.

By any standards Ferrie was a peculiar person. He had a disease that rendered him completely hairless, a condition he tried to disguise by gluing orange tufts of hair, and sometimes even carpet scraps, to his scalp and to the place where his eyebrows would have been. He filled his apartment with thousands of white mice, on which he tested various cancer cures. He was also a pianist and a pornographer, and a bishop in a church in which he was the only member.

Garrison had developed information linking Oswald with Ferrie and a third man, known as either Clem or Clay Bertrand. However, on February 22, 1967, Ferrie's nude, bald body was discovered in his apartment, some eight hours after he had been interviewed by a reporter for the *Washington Post*. An autopsy showed he died from a cerebral hemorrhage resulting from an aneurysm—natural causes, in other words—a diagnosis that was complicated by the fact that Ferrie left behind two handwritten suicide notes.

Ferrie's death left Clay or Clem Bertrand as the only living member of Garrison's assassination triangle. This person had been described to the county investigators as being a young homosexual, about five feet eight inches tall, with sandy hair. The man Garrison eventually indicted was a wealthy and aristocratic New Orleans businessman in his mid-fifties, six feet four inches tall, with stark white hair. His only real link to the case was that he was a homosexual and his name was Clay. Clay Shaw.

Shaw would spend the next two years of his life trying to

clear his name. During that time New Orleans was Assassination Central. Every buff in the country came to town. There was an awestruck feeling that Garrison was peeling the lid off American society; it was as if he had discovered some further dimension of reality, as if he had found the point where parallel lines really did converge, where Ruby and Oswald and Ferrie and Shaw met the Cubans, the Russians, the Pentagon, and the CIA. And Garrison was amazingly self-assured. He gave long interviews in *Playboy* magazine and on the Johnny Carson show detailing the massive conspiracy. He confirmed every suspicion. "My staff and I solved the case months ago," he said breezily. "I wouldn't say this if we didn't have evidence beyond a shadow of a doubt. We know the key individuals, the cities involved, and how it was done."

At the heart of Garrison's theory was the unoriginal notion that Dallas killed Kennedy; the city's millionaire right-wingers financed the plot with the collusion of the Dallas police force and the technical advice of the CIA. These were the witches Garrison hunted. There was also the fashionable idea, added later, that Kennedy was murdered by the military establishment so that it could wage unrestrained war in Vietnam. What made Garrison's investigation so appealing is that he satisfied the profound paranoia of the moment by saying yes, it's true, and it's worse than you thought. Somehow that news came as a relief.

Many of the assassination buffs came to speak at Tulane. New York attorney Mark Lane entangled the Warren Commission in lawyerly webs of contradiction and intrigue. Comedian and activist Dick Gregory spun spooky scenarios of universal government control. He invited us to give a round of applause to the federal agents in the audience tonight, and we cheered ironically, glad to throw aside our naïveté. That was the first time anyone had ever suggested to me that the government thought students were worth keeping an eye on.

When Clay Shaw finally came to trial, one of the witnesses

against him was a Baton Rouge insurance salesman, who said in advance he planned to lie on the stand (because he didn't like Shaw's attorney). Another witness was a heroin addict who said he was sitting on the banks of Lake Pontchartrain, shooting up, when he saw Clay Shaw talking to Lee Harvey Oswald. My favorite prosecution witness was a New York City accountant who had heard Shaw planning the execution of the President. The accountant also admitted that he had been hypnotized frequently—against his will—usually by New York City police officers who were engaged in a Communist conspiracy against him. Part of their scheme was to substitute "dead ringers" for his children during the night, a plot he foiled by fingerprinting his kids every morning at the breakfast table.

New Orleans was the laughingstock of the nation. The conspiracy movement had been gathering energy for years; lightning was bound to strike somewhere, and New Orleans was a natural target. There was a feeling that this travesty could only have happened here, in Oswald's hometown, with a cast of characters only New Orleans could offer. Like Dallas, the entire city was made to feel responsible, an unfair charge that was still too appropriate to deny.

Clay Shaw, who distinguished this episode with grace and humor, died of cancer soon after his acquittal. He had been one of New Orleans's most respected citizens, the managing director of the International Trade Mart, the author of many plays, an expert on Restoration period architecture, whose hobby was rehabilitating French Quarter homes. In World War II he had won the Legion of Merit and the Croix de Guerre. He was a political liberal who had voted for John F. Kennedy. He died, vindicated but ruined, a victim of conspiracy paranoia, queer baiting, and the political ambition of an unscrupulous, and perhaps insane, prosecutor.

For a while it seemed that every conspiracy theorist in the country was working out of Garrison's office. Afterward they scattered in disgrace, with Clay Shaw's reputation, and possibly his death, on their consciences. Of course they later realized that Garrison's investigation had been just another clever scheme to discredit them. It was all part of the great conspiracy, all evidence of witchcraft.

In my sophomore year I fell in love with a redheaded girl who smoked a pipe. I was snaring freshmen for my Cosmopolitan Committee at an open house when Tamzon Feeney walked into my life (as they say in the romantic novels), wearing black stockings and a beige jersey dress. She was as tall as I and more strongly built; I found out later, to my faint disgust, that she had put the shot for a Catholic girls' school in San Diego. Her hair was cut short and combed into bangs, to disguise an unusually long forehead. Her eyes were hazel, and too large; her nose was pug, and too small. She had the usual freckled pallor that accompanies red hair. She was the most beautiful girl I'd ever seen.

There was always about Tamzon an alluring innocence, a part of her nature that the nuns had nearly trapped into a convent, but there was another part that was ready for anything. I never knew anyone who was less afraid of life. While other freshman girls stood about properly cowed and demure, Tamzon entered the room with a look in her eye that suggested she had just gotten shore leave. She watched me for a moment—I was surrounded, for once, by women—then she walked out of the room.

When people say they fell in love at first sight, they usually mean that they saw themselves in another person. What I recognized in Tamzon was a romantic attachment to life that was even greater than mine. We had both suffered restraint in our backgrounds—she by Catholicism, I by growing up in Dallas—but in us that restraint had acted like a drawn bow; when we met we were both in the full flight of release. That was what I saw in her eyes: that there was no dare she would not take, that her life would be lived all the way through—and to hell with convention! On the other hand, I knew from the moment she

233

walked into the room that her hunger was greater than mine, and when she walked away I must have known that she was going to have to break my heart.

She was seventeen. Like many people with excess brains who have raced ahead of their peers, she was oddly immature, and got by largely on bluff and humor. Her most profound secret was that she believed she was called to greatness. She was going to be another Albert Schweitzer or Dr. Tom Dooley. As a result she saw her time in school as a last fling before she disappeared into the jungles and surrendered herself to good works.

On our first date I took her to the French Quarter. Although I had been in New Orleans for only a year myself, I presented the Quarter to Tamzon Feeney as if it were a living thing and mine to give. I took her to Preservation Hall to hear the old black jazzmen; we paid a dollar at the door and sat on the floor, and we could feel the music pounding right through the floorboards and up our spines. This was an obligatory stop for me, although the jazz was fossilized and I felt, as I sat inside the ring of white people in the audience, all of us grinning and tapping our toes, that we were attending a Negro zoo. Afterward, Tamzon and I walked down Chartres Street, to the Napoleon House, the bar of my dreams, a dim old place with dark stains on the wallpaper like Rorschach blots, and a phonograph at which customers picked through the records and played, let's say, "Bolero" or "L'Elsire d'Amore," but the volume was only just loud enough to draw a curtain of sound between the tables, and every table floated in its own isolated pool of candlelight. Redheads are always more beautiful at night, especially in candlelight. A hard look at noon and the colors are all wrong—the hair's gone orangish, the skin is vividly freckled but also translucent and veiny, a kind of 3-D skin—but night brings out the redness and the complexion falls into focus. Here in this atmosphere of excessive romance we told each other about ourselves.

"I am surrounded by hypocrites."

"I know, I know."

"Life is too valuable to be wasted on fools."

"I'm going to change the world."

"I'm going to save it."

Then we laughed a little at our pretension, but the terms were stated. We had been alone forever. We had cultivated our alienation, but we had believed that no one would ever understand us, or even care to. Until now. We looked at each other with relief, and fear.

"Let's get out of here."

I decided to test her. We went for a drive on the levee, where I often went in marginally suicidal moments when I wanted to peer over the edge of life. I owned a 1955 MG roadster, and because it was red, and because the model number, TF 1500, had her initials in it, Tamzon saw it as a kind of chariot for her personality. We put down the top and then lowered the windshield, and the breeze hit us smack in the face. I had never taken a girl riding on the levee before. I turned off the headlights and navigated by moonlight. It was dangerous and famously illegal, but Tamzon was whooping as we flew over dips and bumps. The filthy Mississippi snaked along beside us, filled with gleaming chemicals and the slow commerce of freighters. Then we parked and lay on the grass and listened to the tugboats blast. I was afraid to touch her. Male and female suddenly felt like animals living in different elements, I in the water and she in the air. I thought how strong she was, and how avid. I was already terribly afraid of losing her.

A cop stopped me on the way home. I had forgotten the time—Tamzon was late, she would be punished—but instead of giving me a ticket for speeding, the cop took pity on our predicament and gave us an escort all the way back to Tamzon's dorm. When I walked her to the door and asked for a kiss, she burst into tears.

*　　*　　*

I entered college at a time when the tide of revolution was just beginning to break across the campuses of the nation. I did not picture myself as a part of that tide. I knew that I was part of the Baby Boom, but I had not understood how my generation, by force of numbers, would change the political and cultural life of our nation. I had not seen how society was already arranging itself to accommodate youth. It was part of the solipsism of my own youth to believe that my teenaged taste for hamburgers, for instance, would naturally find expression in the rise of fast-food outlets all over the country, just as my sexual desires would batter down barriers of conduct, and my political beliefs, aimlessly acquired, would change the course of historical events. All of my interests and needs and whims and predilections had enormous consequences, because they were characteristic of millions like me. But I didn't yet understand myself as part of this mass. I didn't foresee our power. I was pleasantly cloistered among the great stone buildings, eager to shut out the world of adults and the world of children, and happy to live among my peers, aged eighteen to twenty-two, in a sort of sexual rhapsody of serious talk and giddy uncoverings and long dizzy afternoons of Kierkegaard and Jax beer.

News reached us nonetheless. Richard Speck, the failed scholar of Woodrow Wilson High School, murdered eight nursing students in Chicago. Charles Whitman, the nation's youngest Eagle Scout, climbed into the tower at the University of Texas and shot forty-four people, killing fourteen. One of the injured students was a high-school classmate of mine. I watched a ceremony on the Quadrangle for the widow of the first Tulane graduate killed in Vietnam. It reminded me that university life was a parenthesis, enclosed on either side by the draft.

But I was in love, and enjoying four years of deferment, and it seemed absurd to worry that this "brushfire war" would be waiting for me on graduation day.

Biographical Notes

Rick Bass was born in Fort Worth and educated at Utah State University. His stories have been collected in *The Watch*. Other books are *The Deer Pasture, Wild to the Heart, Oil Notes, Winter: Notes from Montana,* and *The Ninemile Wolves.* He lives in the Yaak Valley in northern Montana.

Lee Merrill Byrd founded Cinco Puntos Press in El Paso together with her husband, the poet Bobby Byrd. "Major Six Pockets," which describes an actual playhouse fire in which their two sons were burned, won the Texas Institute of Letters Brazos Bookstore Award in 1991. She has published a collection of her stories entitled *My Sister Disappears.*

Diane DeSanders, a poet and former history teacher, was born and raised in Dallas, where she also raised two daughters and earned two degrees from Southern Methodist University. She now lives in New York, where her poems and stories regularly appear in *The Quarterly*.

Mary K. Flatten grew up in San Antonio and graduated from the University of Texas in Austin, where she currently lives. She has worked in advertising and has completed a master's degree in religion at the Episcopal Theological Seminary of the Southwest. "Old Enough" was her first published story.

Robert Flynn, novelist-in-residence at Trinity University, is a native of Chillicothe, Texas. He is the author of *North to Yesterday*, named by *The New York Times* as one of the best books of 1967, and three other novels as well as the nonfiction *A Personal War in Vietnam*. His stories are collected in *Seasonal Rain*.

William Goyen (1916–1983) was born in Trinity, Texas. He wrote novels (including *The House of Breath* and *Arcadio*) as well as poetry, plays, and numerous shorter works. Goyen's *Collected Stories* was nominated for the Pulitzer Prize in 1977.

A. C. Greene's short fiction is collected in *The Highland Park Woman*. Among his twelve other books are *A Personal Country* and *Taking Heart*. He has worked as a columnist and staff writer for *The Dallas Morning News*, *The Dallas Times Herald*, and *The Abilene Reporter News*. Greene, who was born in Abilene, lives now in Salado, Texas.

William Hauptman was born in Wichita Falls, Texas, and graduated from the University of Texas and Yale University. His plays include the Tony Award–winning *Big River*, and he is the author of a novel, *The Storm Chaser*. "Good Rockin' Tonight," the title piece of Hauptman's short story collection, was included in *The Best American Short Stories* of 1982.

Shelby Hearon was born in Kentucky and now lives in New York State but was for many years a resident of Austin, Texas. Among her novels are *Owning Jolene, Group Therapy, A Small Town,* and *Hug Dancing.* She has won numerous grants and awards, including an Ingram Merrill grant, a National Endowment for the Arts creative writing fellowship, and a Guggenheim fellowship.

Larry L. King is the author of the play *The Night Hank Williams Died* and co-author of *The Best Little Whorehouse in Texas,* which was nominated for seven Tony Awards and won two. One of his eleven books, *Confessions of a White Racist,* was nominated for a National Book Award. "Something Went with Daddy" marks his short story debut. King grew up in Texas and lives in Washington, D.C.

Reginald McKnight, who teaches at Carnegie Mellon University in Pittsburgh, attended grade school in Waco, Texas. "The Kind of Light That Shines on Texas," the title story of a collection, received an O. Henry Award and the Kenyon Review New Fiction Prize in 1991. His other books are *Moustapha's Eclipse* (stories) and a novel, *I Get on the Bus.*

Larry McMurtry grew up in Archer City, Texas, the setting for his novels *The Last Picture Show* and *Texasville.* Among his other works are the Pulitzer Prize–winning *Lonesome Dove,* as well as *Terms of Endearment; Horseman, Pass By* (which became the Academy Award–winning film *Hud*); and *The Streets of Laredo.*

Tomás Rivera was born into a migrant farm family in Crystal City, Texas, in 1935. His landmark novel about Chicano migrant workers, *. . . y no se lo tragó la tierra,* was awarded the Quinto Sol Prize and has been translated into English by

Rolando Hinojosa as *This Migrant Earth*. Rivera was chancellor of the University of California at the time of his death in 1984.

Annette Sanford was born in Cuero, Texas, and lives in Ganado. She was a high school English teacher before turning to writing full time. Her stories have appeared in national publications and annual prize collections, including *The Best American Short Stories* and *New Stories from the South*. She has published one collection, *Lasting Attachments*.

C. W. Smith's four novels are *Thin Men of Haddam, Country Music, The Vestal Virgin Room*, and *Buffalo Nickel*. He's also the author of an autobiography, *Uncle Dad*. He lives in Dallas, where he is a professor of English at Southern Methodist University.

Lynna Williams was born in Waco but grew up in Fort Worth and Abilene. Her stories are collected in *Things Not Seen*. Her first novel is *The Province of Love*. She teaches English and creative writing at Emory University in Atlanta.

Bryan Woolley was born in Gorman, Texas. He was educated at Texas Western College (now the University of Texas at El Paso), Texas Christian University, and Harvard. He has published four novels and four works of nonfiction, of which the most recent is *The Bride Wore Crimson*. He has had a long career as a journalist and is currently a staff writer for *The Dallas Morning News*.

Lawrence Wright is the author of four books: *City Children, Country Summer; In the New World: Growing Up with America, 1960–1984; Saints and Sinners;* and *Remembering Satan*. He is a staff writer for *The New Yorker* magazine. He was born in Dallas and lives in Austin.

Kay Cattarulla holds degrees from Cornell and Columbia universities. After an early career in book publishing in New York, she lived for ten years in Europe, South America, and the Middle East, accompanying her husband, Elliot, an executive with Exxon Corporation. On their return to New York in the seventies, she allied herself with a group of performing artists in a pioneering community theater on the Upper West Side. She worked for twelve years for that organization, Symphony Space, and in 1985 originated the nationally known literary series "Selected Shorts," in which actors read short fiction to a live audience. In 1990 the Cattarullas moved to Dallas, and in 1992 Kay founded the "Arts and Letters Live" literary series. The Cattarullas have one son, John.

Also from Southern Methodist University Press

Texas Bound
8 by 8: Stories by Texas Writers, Read by Texas Actors

A boxed set of two 90-minute audiocassettes containing eight stories from the anthology:

> Larry McMurtry's "There Will Be Peace in Korea,"
>   read by Tommy Lee Jones
> William Goyen's "The Texas Principessa," read by
>   Doris Roberts
> Robert Flynn's "The Midnight Clear," read by
>   Tess Harper
> Reginald McKnight's "The Kind of Light That
>   Shines on Texas," read by Tyress Allen
> Lynna Williams's "Personal Testimony," read by
>   Judith Ivey
> Tomás Rivera's "Picture of His Father's Face," read
>   by Roger Alvarez
> Annette Sanford's "Trip in a Summer Dress," read
>   by Norma Moore
> Lawrence Wright's "Escape," read by Randy Moore

Host: Tess Harper. Produced by Kay Cattarulla. Directed by Randy Moore.
ISBN 0-87074-369-4

Available at bookstores or from:
Southern Methodist University Press
Drawer C
College Station, Texas 77843
Toll-free order number: 1-800-826-8911
FAX 409-847-8752